D0840350

MOVING OUT!
A Young Adult's Guide to Living on Your Own

CINDY BABYN

GSPH

GENERAL STORE PUBLISHING HOUSE
499 O'Brien Road, Box 415
Renfrew, Ontario, Canada K7V 4A6
Telephone 1.613.432.7697 or 1.800.465.6072
www.gsph.com

ISBN 978-1-897508-95-4

Copyright © Cindy Babyn 2011

Cover art, design, formatting: Magdalene Carson
Printed by Custom Printers of Renfrew Ltd., Renfrew, Ontario
Printed and bound in Canada

No part of this book may be reproduced, stored in a retrieval system, or transmitted in any form or by any means without the prior written permission of the publisher or, in case of photocopying or other reprographic copying, a licence from Access Copyright (Canadian Copyright Licensing Agency), 1 Yonge Street, Suite 1900, Toronto, Ontario, M5E 1E5.

Library and Archives Canada Cataloguing in Publication

Babyn, Cindy,

Moving out! : a young adult's guide to living on your own / Cindy Babyn.

ISBN 978-1-897508-95-4

1. Young adults--Life skills guides. 2. Life skills--Handbooks, manuals,

etc. I. Title.

HQ799.5.B33 2010   646.700842   C2010-904928-4

First printing, January 2011
Second printing, July 2011

This book is dedicated to:

My niece Jacklyn and my nephew Jake

Family and friends
who have helped me move way too many times

My grandmother, who always believed that
someday we'd be rich and famous

As well as to all the courageous young people
moving out and living on their own.

Contents

Acknowledgements

Writing this book has been a really fun project. I would like to thank all of those individuals who worked with me to make it happen, including:

My publisher, Tim Gordon of General Store Publishing House, for taking a chance on a new author and being okay with publishing a book that's "super-Canadiana"

My editor, Jane Karchmar, for keeping everything tight and for patiently teaching me a few things along the way about English grammar

Mag Carson for her cool book design and illustrations

Alison Roesler, publicist, for making a great effort to get distribution deals

Lieutenant Arthur Herscovitch, Fire Prevention Officer, and Captain Marc Messier, Information Officer, both of the Ottawa Fire Services, for providing me with additional recommendations and reviewing and approving the fire safety and prevention tips included in this book

Friends and family who reviewed book drafts, gave me additional content ideas, and encouraged me along the way.

Special Note:

Actual stories from a variety of individuals about moving, including moving in with and living with roommates, are placed throughout this book. Some names and cities have been changed. Thanks to all those people who were brave enough to share their moving stories with us.

Preface

Moving Out! *A Young Adult's Guide to Living on Your Own* was written for the young person moving out to live on his/her own for the first time (or the first few times), as well as for the parents and guardians who are supporting the preparedness of their young adult children as they make their way in the world and begin to live independently in one of our great Canadian cities.

I have lived on my own a fairly long time and I've moved almost twenty times (that I can remember)! This experience, acquired in a wide variety of locations and apartments (from living with room-mates in houses and a high-rise condo, to renting floors of flats-style houses; renting a coach house, living in a new housing development, living in a house on a dirt road in farming country, to renting self-contained apartments in houses in the ultra neighbourhoody-neigh-bourhoods), has given me some perspective and knowledge to share about moving and living on your own that might make your life just a little easier than it was for me.

This book is organized into three parts:

Part I:
The practical aspects of moving and living on your own successfully

Part II:
The emotional and social aspects of living on your own

Part III:
Income tax, eco-friendly choices, and principles for living on your own in a big Canadian city

Letter to the Reader

Dear Reader:

Most people would probably agree that the age a person moves out of his or her family home for the first time is totally dependent on a wide variety of factors, such as level of personal maturity, financial status, and the degree of the person's desire to be brave enough to move out on his/her own. Sometimes heading off to university or college is a pretty clear marker for many young adults.

In my case, I moved out when I was young — likely younger than most. I was seventeen and I was unhappy. I tried to pretend that everything was okay and I tried to keep quiet about my feelings. All I knew was that living at home was not working out for me and I was tired of the stress. I was praying for the day I could move out. Thankfully I had a lot of really good friends who helped keep my spirits high through those days. They gave me a third-party perspective on what I was going through and they gave me a lot of emotional support.

After school one day, I found myself with some friends in a café on Yonge Street in Toronto, having coffee and croissants. One of my friends told me that she was going to ask her mom and dad if I could move in with them, since her older sister had just moved out. When my friend said those words, the idea of it became a possibility and it started to feel real. It seemed like it could actually happen. Although I was relieved and excited by the idea, I was kind of afraid. I was afraid of the moment when I would tell my foster mom that I was going to move out.

My friend spoke to her parents, and to my surprise they actually agreed to talk with me about allowing me to live there. So we arranged a meeting. Although I had seen her parents on the street from time to time, I didn't actually know them. When I got to my friend's house, we all sat in their living room and talked about what I was going through at home. Her parents offered to take me in for a trial period and thought that we should have family meetings about once a month to see how it was all going and to gauge whether any adjustments were necessary. Our agreement was that I would pay them a small amount each month to support my food costs. I also had to agree to follow the house rules, mostly concerning curfew, and that I had to help out with house chores. I agreed to those things without any hesitation.

So I went home and I told my foster mom that I was going to move out. I got permission from the Children's Aid Society to leave before I was eighteen, the age until which by law I was supposed to remain in care.

I moved in with my friend and her family. I had a room on the top floor. Oddly enough, it had a little sink, which was handy for washing my hair. I ate meals with my friend and her family and had many amazing conversations with them. The best way I can say it is that they "felt like my people." They were well-educated. They were artistically inclined. They were fairly liberal in thought and free-spirited. They were politically engaged. They shared their thoughts and feelings and ideas with each other. They laughed. They supported each other and they totally welcomed me in. I learned, in the presence of these adults and my friend, how to relax and be myself at home, although it took me a long time to open up and trust that it was okay to do so. For me, this was a great gift. It was an amazing experience to enjoy being at home with people.

About a year and a half later, the day came when I was going to start first-year university. I was nineteen. I decided it was going to be a lot easier to live downtown. I found a place advertised on a sign at the faculty where I was going to study. I rented a partially furnished room on the third floor of a house in a neighbourhood with a good vibe. It was within walking distance of the university. There was no lease — I just paid month-to-month. The room had a single bed and a desk with a chair. It had a tiny balcony that overlooked a mature, tree-lined street. It was a beautiful view. I brought a bookcase, my books, and my clothes. I had a lock on my door and I shared a kitchen on the second floor with the other tenant, who ended up being my very good friend. I brought some of my own kitchenware, including a German-made espresso-maker, which, amazingly, still works today! My friend and I were a good pair and we didn't have any problems sharing the kitchen. We often cooked and ate together when our schedules matched. After this first year of university was over, I went off to study in Rotterdam, Holland, where I ended up moving four times in two years. Do you see a pattern emerging here? I move a lot!

So, there you have a glimpse of the stories of the first couple of moves on my own. Both were really great in their own ways. Given my life experience, I became a person who ensures that I am happy at home, wherever my home might be and whomever it might be with, because as the famous saying goes, "home is where the heart is." I believe that's a very true statement, and I always strive to achieve it.

I am guessing that many young adults move out of very supportive homes and families that they enjoy as they make their way in the world. If you have a family that you enjoy being with, I would advise you to think about the positive aspects of staying at home for as long as you are able to. It is super-expensive and not exactly easy to try and make it out there on your own, especially if you are trying to get a university or college degree or your first home. Save up while you can! On the other hand, it can be a very rewarding experience to move out. You get an opportunity to learn and grow a lot. The bottom line is to trust your own feelings about what is right for you.

Today I can look back and say that I have enjoyed all the moves I've made. They have each brought new experiences, new ideas, new environments, and new people into my life. I hope that some of the advice I'm sharing in this guide will make sense to you, will help you, and that you'll have many of your own great experiences. Good luck!

— *Cindy Babyn*

PART I

The Practical Aspects of Moving and Living on Your Own Successfully

 # Some of the Positives of Living on Your Own

In your own space . . .

- You can come and go as you please without having to "report" or inform anybody of where you're going and what time you'll be home.

- You don't have to clean up anybody else's mess and no one will nag you about your own mess!

- You don't have to listen to anybody else's humming, singing, instrument playing, pen clicking, annoying jokes, opinions, or fights.

- You can watch whatever TV show you want to without having to check anyone else's plan or preference.

- You don't have to wait for anyone else to get out of the bathroom!

- All the closet and counter space is yours.

- You can stay up as late as you want without worrying that you'll disturb anyone else.
- You can dance like nobody's watching because nobody is!
- You can listen to music that you like when you want to without worrying that it has to suit someone else's taste or mood.
- You can go to bed as early as you want without having to cope with other people's noise while you're trying to go to sleep.
- You can cook according to your own tastes, taste your cooking, and dip the spoon right back in without rinsing it off!
- You can have the furniture, art work, paint colours, decorations, kitchenware, plants, etc., according to your own taste.
- You can have a pet without worrying about anyone else's allergies.
- You only have to do your own laundry.
- You can have the freedom and the space to develop into the person you want to become without others watching you and challenging your decisions and actions as you experiment and grow.

 # Some of the Negatives of Living on Your Own

- You will pay 100 percent of the costs (rent, utilities, phone, cable, parking, etc.).
- It can get lonely to come home to an empty, quiet, home or apartment.
- If you hear a bump in the night and get scared, you are going to have to have the courage to get up and investigate it by yourself.
- If you see a spider, wasp, other bug, or rodent in your space, you are either going to have to catch and release it or kill it by yourself.
- If you get sick and don't have medical supplies, it is you who will have to drag your sick self out to the store to get them.
- No one will be there to make a meal for you, help you clean up, or find anything.
- If you travel, you will have to make alternative arrangements for people to take care of your pet, water your plants, or pick up your mail while you're gone.

Apartment/Home Hunting

Definitions of Types of Apartments

While there may be some variations, the descriptions below generally hold true.

SHARED: You typically rent your bedroom and share the kitchen, bathroom, and living room with others who are either the landlords or other renters/roommates. This is usually the cheapest option.

ROOMING HOUSE: Exactly the same as the Shared description above.

BACHELOR: One room (where you sleep, cook, and eat), plus a separate bathroom, which is exclusively yours to use. A bachelor apartment may have its own private entrance; or you might have to share an entryway with others (like a hallway).

ONE-BEDROOM: Bedroom, separate kitchen (sometimes combined with a dining area), a living room, and one bathroom.

TWO-TO-FOUR BEDROOMS: Same as above, with extra bedrooms and sometimes more than one bathroom. Larger numbers of bedrooms may mean that you are renting a house with access to the basement, garage, and backyard (if applicable).

UNFURNISHED APARTMENT: You bring all the furniture and kitchenware.

SEMI-FURNISHED: The apartment has some but not all furniture (more expensive).

FURNISHED: Most expensive — it likely has all furniture and kitchenware.

SUITE is another word often used as a substitute for apartment because some landlords placing an ad think it sounds classier. One-bedroom apartment and one-bedroom suite both refer to the same thing.

Quebec Terminology for Apartments

Descriptions of apartments in Quebec look very unusual to renters in other parts of Canada. Apartments advertised here are identified by a number system comprising whole and half numbers. The whole number refers to the total number of rooms (bedroom, kitchen, living room = 3 rooms). The "half" number refers to a bathroom. Therefore,

1 1/2 = Bachelor apartment with a bathroom

2 1/2 = One bedroom, a dine-in kitchen, and a bathroom

3 1/2 = One bedroom, a dine-in kitchen, a living room, and a bathroom

4 1/2 = Two bedrooms, a dine-in kitchen, a living room, and a bathroom. If there is more than one bathroom, it will be specified separately in the text description.

5 1/2 = Three bedrooms, a living room, a dine-in kitchen, and a bathroom. If there is more than one bathroom, it will be specified separately in the text description.

"APPARTEMENT" refers to an apartment in a high-rise apartment building.

"LOGEMENT" refers to an apartment in a house (e.g., where each floor has its own apartment).

ere is a list of things to think about when looking for your next residence:

- Can you afford it?
- Are hydro (electricity) and utilities (natural gas) charges included or extra?
- Is there a lease agreement you have to sign, locking you in for a specified time period (typically one year)?
- Do you intuitively get a "good vibe" from the space?
- Does the space feel like "you"?
- Can you imagine yourself enjoying living here?

- If you need it, is there a permanent parking spot? Is there an additional parking fee? Is there a place to store your winter/summer tires in the off-season?

- Are you close to the public transit stop? Is it too close? In other words, are you going to have to suck in bus fumes if the window is open in the summer? Are you going to have to listen to bad bus brakes or streetcar screech, especially on rainy days?

- Are you right on a high-traffic road? Will the noise or constant movement outside bother you?

- Does the space meet your physical accessibilities needs or those of a friend/family member with mobility issues who may want to visit you?

- Do you have indoor access to laundry facilities? If not, is there a laundromat close by? Remember that carting heavy laundry through the snow or rain is a big drag if you don't have a car.

- Is it a basement or first-floor apartment with inhabited floors overhead? This can mean that you will likely hear people walking above you. Sometimes this can be very loud.[1]

- Are there noise rules, such as a required quiet hour like eleven p.m.? Are you okay with respecting that?

- Is it near a restaurant? Be careful about renting above or beside restaurants or street-side markets because they are more prone to insect or rodent infestations. In these locations, the landlord should inform you about any of these issues, tell you the pest control plan and whether s/he will pay to resolve any future problems.

- Is your place ultra close to a fire station or hospital where you'll often be hearing vehicle sirens at all hours of the day and night?

- Is it across the street from an electrical station? Some people feel that electrical grids affect their health negatively.

- Does your space have air conditioning? Remember that higher floors can often be very hot in the summer. If there is air conditioning and you have to pay for hydro (electricity), find out

---

1   It is useful to check multi-resident apartments (such as flats-style, condos, or apartment buildings) while other residents are at home. Listen to whether television, radio, newborn baby crying, or others playing musical instruments is creating more noise than you can bear.

how much it has cost the previous tenants on their electricity bill during the summer.

- Can you control your own heat? What type of heating is it? Baseboard heat is really expensive if you have to pay a separate hydro charge above your rent.
- Are you allowed to paint the place using the colours you want? (Ask the landlord.)
- Is the place in good repair (such as working windows; taps that don't drip; sinks that don't clog; working fridge, stove, and oven)?
- Does the space smell clean (e.g., no lingering cigarette smoke smell or mildew)?
- Is it bright enough? Are there enough windows?
- Do the ceilings feel high enough (especially important for basement units)?
- Who does the snow shovelling? Will it be you? Is there a very large walk to clear?
- Are there a thousand stairs you have to climb to get to the front door (while carrying your grocery bags or that you'll have to shovel in the winter . . .)?
- Are you okay with taking an elevator home? If the elevator is out of service, are you okay with taking the stairs? Is the dwelling you're looking at close to the emergency exits (stairs)? Could the fire department's exterior ladder reach to that height to free you?
- Is there a place to store your bike, protected from the rain and snow?
- Is there enough closet space?
- Are there smoke detectors? The landlord needs to ensure there are smoke detectors on every floor of the residence and one outside of every bedroom.
- Do you have a carbon monoxide detector? It can save your life.
- Is there a toilet plunger next to the toilet? In an emergency, it's a major must-have.
- Are you within walking distance to stores?
- How long is the commute time from home to work or school? Try to keep this at a minimum.

Neighbourhoods

Experienced taxi drivers have an amazing knowledge regarding neighbourhood qualities, characteristics, and safety. Consider taking a ride and striking up a conversation with your cabbie as a means of intelligence gathering. Otherwise, ask friends, family, or college/ university student housing representatives if they have advice about which neighbourhoods are safe, cool, and convenient, and which neighbourhoods to avoid. Getting advice is especially helpful if you're checking options in a neighbourhood you're unfamiliar with or a new city, province, or territory.

If you are a person who doesn't have a car, you may want to live in a place where you are within walking distance to everything you need. The most vibrant urban neighbourhoods are typically the most expensive and relatively safe compared to other parts of the city. They have a high diversity of stores and services, and you'll typically find a lot of people walking around or cycling in these neighbourhoods, which gives them a healthy sense of community. Living here will mean that the rent is higher for a smaller space, but it will likely have a great urban vibe and you'll have ready access to the highest number of the following:

- Grocery store
- Farmers' market
- Bakery
- Butcher shop
- Health food store
- Pharmacy
- Dry cleaners
- Dollar Store
- Bicycle sales and repair shop
- Bicycle lanes and bike lock stations
- Post office
- Hardware store
- Public benches
- Gift shops
- Clothing stores
- Second-hand store
- Restaurants and great brunch places
- Video store
- Movie theatre
- Hairdresser and aesthetics salon
- Laundromat
- Shoe repair
- Coffee shop
- Photocopy shop or drugstore with a photocopier/fax
- Internet café
- Liquor or beer store
- Library

- Bookstore; used bookstore
- Music stores (CD, vinyl, instrument sales)
- A local newspaper
- Neighbourhood Watch program
- A walk-in medical clinic
- A dental clinic
- A gym
- A bank
- A commercial arts and crafts gallery
- Art supply store
- Music, dance, or craft education centre
- Public school
- Daycare centre
- Multiple public transit stops
- A gas station
- Oil change and mechanic garage
- Adequate street parking
- Good street lighting
- Christmas lighting on the streets in winter
- A park, local outdoor pool and tennis court
- A high number and variety of trees
- Well-tended residential gardens
- Dandelions (sign of an absence of pesticides)
- A fire station close by
- High volume of people walking and cycling
- Residents sitting on porches, talking to neighbours, sweeping the sidewalk
- Store-front tax return service during taxation season (like H & R Block®)

Where Apartments Are Advertised

- Neighbourhood community newspapers
- "Apartment for Rent" signs in front of apartment buildings or houses
- College or university bulletin boards
- For a dormitory room, speak with the staff of the college or university you are planning to attend
- The Internet: Web site *www.viewit.ca* (nice because these apartments have photos — you get a sense before you get there!)
- Google "Easy Roommate," which has photos of shared accommodation spaces and potential roommates
- Major city or national newspapers, which advertise apartments, but these are usually the most expensive and beyond the price range of a young adult starting out

I found an ad at UBC to rent a room in a house in swanky Shaughnessy Heights. This place was huge. My bedroom was as big as whole apartments I've rented elsewhere. I shared the bathroom and kitchen with the homeowners, and they often cooked meals for me. They never cared about my comings and goings and they themselves often travelled for months at a time, so it was like I had my very own mansion. The whole experience was kind of like a fairy tale. They actually cried when I moved out.

Dawn Sandy
Vancouver, B.C.

The Frustrations of Apartment Hunting

Rarely will you find the apartment you love and can afford within your first two or three viewing appointments. Sometimes apartments sound fantastic in an advertisement, but you just won't believe how many crappy and disgusting apartments there are out there, especially when you don't have a lot of money to spend. Try to factor in some time to look at a number of places and bring along your patience — you'll probably need it!

"...with a lovely view of the Gatineau Hills..."

Living in Residence on a College or University Campus

Many youth find that moving into "residence" at their college or university is a great transition option when they leave home. A residence is typically a large building like an apartment complex. There are tons of other people around, so it's not lonely. Students can pay for basic shelter consisting of a room with a bed, closet, desk, and phone — often shared with one other person. Everyone uses the common bathrooms, showers, and kitchen. If you are not much of a cook, you can buy a meal plan on-site.

In a way, living in residence is a bit like going to camp. There are adults who make sure nothing gets too out of hand in the dorm rooms. There are student newcomer guides, older students you can talk to for advice, social activities, and study groups. It is also convenient because you won't have to deal with commuting. You'll be close to the library, gym, laundry facilities, and — most important — your classes! The hardest part is probably going to be learning how to live with very few possessions because not much is going to fit into your room!

I left home to go to university and ended up renting my own room in residence. Half were freshmen and the other half were upper-year and graduate-level students. There were no rules about noise — it was kind of like anarchy. While it was generally noisy chaos, I started to notice people looking at me funny in the shared kitchen. The problem became obvious when the resident Don approached me to tell me that there had been complaints against my flute practising. I only practised for about one hour each day, at seven in the evening, and I was pretty good. Still, I was getting the boot. The Don gave me the keys to a large chapel-type room for my practising. It had wooden panels and a vaulted ceiling, and the acoustics were amazing. I've never forgotten how cool it was to practise there. The looks from my dorm-mates immediately ceased. It was happy times all around!

Crystal
Toronto, Ontario

For my third year of university, I ended up sharing an on-campus university apartment with three other guys. My parents helped me move in there. One of the guys actually told me that it made him a bit sad to see us have our parents help because he missed his dad, who had passed away recently. He was nice to have around because he had a really cute girlfriend he liked to impress, so when she was coming over he would make our whole apartment spotlessly clean. We liked it when she came over, just for that, and we always tried to encourage her to come over as often as she wanted so we could avoid having to deal with our own mess!

When we moved in, we each contributed some items to make the house livable. One of the guys brought a couch for the living room. It was from his grandmother and it was nasty! It was orange and had flowers on it—not exactly a guys' design style. Still, none of us even bothered to make the effort to put a sheet over it. When I left that apartment, I actually took that gaudy couch with me. I didn't have much money, so as ugly as it was, I kind of needed it. I ended up keeping it for four years and then turfed it out on the lawn for someone else to pick up. It was actually gone by the next morning, so who knows how much more of the world that couch has seen!

François
Montreal, Quebec

When I was eighteen, I moved into residence. It was a tiny room. The girl I was paired up with was really nice. By November I was feeling kind of homesick so I liked the constant company of others in my res. It was also my birthday that month. My roommate totally decorated our room and got me a birthday cake. It was one of the best birthdays I ever had! In the second semester I was getting more concerned about trying to pull up my grades but it was kind of hard with people coming over all the time. One girl actually ended up sleeping in our room because her roommate always had her boyfriend over and she couldn't stand listening to them making out all the time. So my roommate and I put our beds together and the three of us girls slept on this makeshift double bed. Believe me when I say this wasn't my idea. I really needed my own space and *a good sleep. In general I found it a bit hard to be independent in residence. If you were going out and someone didn't have a plan, all of a sudden your plan was their plan. While there were a lot of positives about living in residence, one year was all I could take. I needed my space and got housing off campus for my second year.*

Brooke
Ottawa, Ontario

I grew up in a small town in New Brunswick where my family didn't share the same level of interest in fishing and hunting as most others in my community. Instead, my dad gave me a strong interest in political engagement, and we sometimes attended political rallies together. My mom sparked a passion for arts and culture within me, particularly for theatre. So I really wanted to go and see more of the world. My friends, who were more into traditional leisure, didn't quite understand me and thought I was being a bit pretentious about wanting to leave.

Anyway, when I was eighteen I got a job in Ottawa as a page at the House of Commons. I moved out with just one suitcase and flew on a military airplane from Halifax. When I arrived, I was settled into the Thompson Dorm at Ottawa U, and shortly after my arrival everything got stolen except a few of my clothes. I ended up being transferred into the Leblanc Dorm with other francophone people, which was nice because I didn't speak much English at the time. Although they spoke French, it was a bit of a cultural shock because I was Acadian and these people were Franco-Ontarian. I remember being mad because they wanted to watch Star Trek in English while my La Petite Vie show was on at the same time. "These people aren't French!" I thought.

My parents had been pretty supportive of me, so I didn't have basic living-on-my-own skills by the time I left home. I remember taking my clothes to the residence laundromat and not knowing what to do. I didn't know if you put the water first, or the soap, or the clothes, but some ladies helped me out. I liked living in residence because I needed to take things step by step. Although our dorm room was seriously cramped for studying, I just wasn't ready to deal with finding an apartment and setting up my own telephone line and hydro service. I also didn't want to have to lock myself into a one-year lease and have to figure out how to sublet it in the summer months when my university year was finished.

Ghislain
Val–Comeau, New Brunswick

I found housing on campus for my first year of university. I ended up sharing an apartment with another girl from a well-to-do family. I was a struggling student who tended to buy multiple items when they were on sale (like shampoo or toothpaste). I started to get the feeling that my things were disappearing, as well as some of my cash. I just always seemed to be short and I found myself going to the bank more often. Since we didn't have many people over, I obviously started to suspect my roommate. One day I got out of the shower early to check and see if there was any nefarious business going on in my room and I actually caught my roommate red-handed stealing from my purse! She was totally mortified and had no ready-made excuse. Because I couldn't trust her any longer, I gave my landlord notice and moved out six weeks later. The only bright side to this story is that when I lived at this location, I actually bumped into a man whom I really liked who also lived in the neighbourhood. After dating for a while, we married and we are still together. All you single ladies: take note, there's still hope out there! You just never know when or where you're going to meet your man . . .

Jacquie
Winnipeg, Manitoba

Checking Out Apartments
— the Competition for a Residential Space

When you rent an apartment, the homeowner or property manager renting you the space is called "the landlord," and you are going to be called "the tenant." You will likely face a lot of competition from others, as a landlord doesn't have to select just anyone to be a tenant. Landlords typically meet a lot of interested candidates, run background checks on prospective tenants, and pick the person they like best and who they believe will respect their property and pay the rent in full and on time.

When You Meet a Landlord, You Will Have to Convey That:

- You have enough money to afford the place

- You are eager to move in (having your first and last month's cheque ready can sometimes tip the scales in your favour)

- You have good personal references (such as a character reference from a friend, mentor or teacher, or parent or guardian)

- You have a work reference to prove that you have a job and that you are a good employee

BE SURE TO DRESS APPROPRIATELY WHEN VIEWING A POTENTIAL HOMESTEAD — with nice, clean clothing and good personal hygiene. You need to make the best first impression you can, one that exudes confidence and conveys that you are trustworthy and reasonably "normal" — whatever that is! Make sure that you are on time. If the landlord is the one who shows up late, don't complain about it to his/her face. Be as patient, gracious, and understanding as you can. This might be your future landlord.

As a matter of personal security, as well as having a second opinion about a space from a person you trust, **IT IS SMART TO CHECK OUT POTENTIAL APARTMENTS WITH A FRIEND.** Make sure this person is well-dressed and behaves well on-site, too. Chew gum before your visit (for fresh breath), or after your visit if you're an avid gum-chewer. A stranger might find it offensive; or may think you are not so intelligent, particularly if he or she is having trouble understanding what you're saying while you're chewing your gum!

Rental Application Form

Sometimes a prospective landlord will immediately like you, trust you, and decide he or she wants you as a tenant, which is ideal. Others will actually hand you an application form to fill out. At the very least, most landlords usually check out where you have lived before to research whether you've paid your rent in full and on time, or that your parent/guardian believes you can financially afford to rent the place. Some may run a credit check on you to make sure you have a good track record of paying your bills and loan payments on time (if applicable). Accept the rental form calmly and fill it out on-site, outside, or in a nearby coffee shop if you really like the place and have all the information required. If you get a sixth sense that you don't trust the landlord, or that some of the questions appear to be "phishing" for far too much personal information, trust your instincts and do not submit the form. Simply take it and advise the person that you have another appointment to get to (then don't submit it and look elsewhere).

Congratulations! You've Got a Place — Now What?

Keeping up excellent relations with your landlord is important because, when you move the next time, your potential new landlord will likely call your current landlord to find out what kind of tenant you were. (Were you reliable? Did you pay your rent on time? Did you keep things tidy? Were you pleasant? Were you respectful?)

Rental/Lease Agreement

Your new landlord may ask you to sign a Rental/Lease Agreement so that there is a clear business arrangement made in writing between you and the landlord. Some landlords don't provide a rental agreement because it is not an actual requirement, but it can be a handy tool to clarify everything. A rental agreement is a document that usually identifies:

- The move-in date
- The amount of the rent
- The day of the month that your rent money is due to the landlord
- Whether this is a weekly rental agreement (rare), a month-to-month, or a one-year agreement (both of these are very typical)
- Whether your landlord prefers cash or a cheque
- Whether the landlord requires a number of post-dated cheques in advance (for example, perhaps you will be asked to provide cheques dated January 1, February 1, and March 1, then provide

the next set of cheques dated April 1, May 1, and June 1, etc.; this way, your landlord will not have to chase you for your cheques, especially if your schedules are very different)

- A record of giving the landlord a deposit (most typically the amount of the last month's rent right up front at the beginning)

- How much notice you are required to give the landlord if you want to move somewhere else (this is usually thirty days, but sometimes it is sixty days; this will give the landlord time to advertise his or her rental unit and to make any necessary repairs or upgrades between tenants)

Should you sign a rental agreement, both you and the landlord will each sign it to demonstrate that both parties agree to its terms. Each of you will retain a copy for your records. Signing a lease will mean that you agree to pay the rent for the duration of the entire period of the agreement.

I needed to find a new place to live when my landlord sold his house. I had to pay first and last month's rent at the beginning and I signed a one-year lease for a rooming house. Two guys shared the main floor. I had my own bedroom and washroom on the second floor, and a lady lived on the top floor in the master suite. Together we all shared the living room and dining room.

On the very first day that I moved into the apartment, one of the guys from the main floor helped me figure out where the nearest bank was. I noticed that he was cute. As time passed, I really started to like this guy, but all my family and friends warned me not to date my roommate because they said it was going to be really hard if we broke up and were still trying to live in the same house. Although I appreciated their advice, it didn't work for me, so we started dating. All I can say is, when it's right, it's right. We lived in that apartment, dating for six years, and then he proposed to me! We moved out so that as a married couple we could have our own space. So far, we've been happily married for an additional five years! I thank my lucky stars for having found that apartment — it came with a husband!

Gail
Toronto, Ontario

Subletting Your Apartment When You Have Signed a Lease Agreement

If you are a university or college student who has signed a one-year lease for an apartment close to your school, what are you going to do if you want to move back home over the summer to save money? Or what if you are just a renter who will be moving to a different city for a job? You might want to try and sublet your apartment.

As a rule of thumb, you have to get permission from your landlord to sublet the apartment or room to someone else. The landlord may have done a background check on you, and if he or she is open to the idea of subletting, he or she might want to do a background check on the person you have in mind for the sublet. The landlord might also want you to continue to be financially responsible for the rent being paid in full and on time during those months, if you expect to return to the place following your absence.

If you are simply subletting your room, and other roommates are staying behind, remember to get approval from the roommates as well. You don't want to make your co-residents angry at having to put up with someone they don't like!

If you will be returning following the sublet period, consider clearing out all of your stuff to make room for the new resident and to make sure none of your things go missing while you are gone. You might also want to take photographs of your space to have a record of its condition when the person moved in; be sure you both put your initials on the prints. This might cover you if you have to take the person to small claims court if he/she has behaved recklessly and damaged the place.

I was renting an apartment with my boyfriend, but then we broke up, so I had to look for a new place. On the Craig's List Web site, I found an affordable four-month sublet option in a low-rise apartment building, sharing with three others. During the first week, the other roommates were really nice, and I was happy that I chose this place. Then they had a party on the weekend that got pretty out of hand. I was going to talk to them about it but I figured it was just a weekend thing. I was wrong. These roommates had people over seven days a week. People would show up at our place around eleven p.m. and party until five-thirty a.m. It was brutal, because my work shift started at 8:00 a.m., so I was getting practically no sleep. There was no reasoning with these people.

One night, while I was trying to sleep in my room, I actually heard one of the partiers asking if anyone had any more coke (cocaine). I was scared of who my roommates were letting into our apartment so I put a lock on the inside and outside of my bedroom door to prevent strangers from trying to take their party into my room at night, or to try and steal my stuff. I was exhausted from getting virtually no sleep so I changed my sleeping schedule to be from five p.m., when I got home from work, to eleven p.m., when their parties started.

My immune system really started to plummet due to the lack of sleep and the weird sleeping and eating schedule I had adopted. Although this place was in a pretty good neighbourhood, I found out later that it was a "bad" apartment building, known to the police. One time the police were inside my building and they asked me to actually prove that I lived in an apartment there, which I did. This was a total nightmare renting experience. I stuck it out for the four months and then moved somewhere else.

Dana
Ottawa, Ontario

Rent Receipts

Your landlord may give you rent receipts, which is a simple form to show that he/she has received your rent money that month. Some don't provide receipts. One reason you might find it important to ask for rent receipts is if you ever declare on your income tax return that you paid rent and you get audited by the Canada Revenue Agency (CRA) and they ask you to show these receipts. In most cases, it does not make sense to declare to the CRA that you paid rent. Ask a tax professional whether declaring that you paid rent has some tax advantage for you (more about taxes and tax returns in Part III of this book).

Establishing Your Credibility and Trustworthiness as a Responsible Tenant

- Always pay your rent in full and on time. If you know that you are going to experience a problem, try to borrow money from someone you know and pay the rent as if you are not having any problem whatsoever. If that fails, speak candidly to the landlord explaining the situation. Sometimes together you can come up with an arrangement she/he can agree to. Some provinces and territories have an established late-charge penalty fee.

- Make sure the exterior of your place looks presentable (swept, no garbage accumulation, etc.).

- Respect all of the landlord's rules, such as those concerning noise.

- When you move, make sure that you keep your previous landlord's name and phone number, in a place you can find it, in case your next prospective landlord asks for a reference.

The first apartment I ever moved into was with guys I had been friends with for fourteen years. We were all really excited about moving out and getting our first place together. We rented the basement and first floor of a duplex. Two of the rooms were a good size, and two rooms were not much bigger than closets. Three of us fought over who was going to get the biggest rooms. One friend didn't care and he opted for one of the small rooms. My other friend decided he would live in the living room on the main floor, but it didn't have a door, so he decided to make a door. His dad was really good at building stuff so he came over and helped my friend make a door.

One day, our landlord came over and noticed the new door. He was really mad and he threatened to take legal action against us if we made any other modifications to his house. My roommate was forced to pay a contractor $1,000 to reverse the changes, and we learned that we'd better never make modifications again before speaking to the landlord first.

Scott
Ottawa, Ontario

Landlord and Tenant Dispute Resolution Services

— Helping You When You Have Problems with the Landlord

*T*here are branches within provincial/territorial government departments that can provide renters with information on their rights and general renting regulations. They can also be an ear for you to explain disputes with your landlord to see if you are in the right or not. Although some dispute resolution services are free, most provinces/territories charge a small fee to review your case (anywhere from ten dollars to forty-five dollars). See Appendix A for the service access information in your area.

A Bad Landlord

As a renter, if you feel the landlord is not behaving properly toward you, you may be right. Sometimes you might encounter a new landlord who does not know the rules about being a good landlord. You could refer the landlord to the landlord and tenant services in your area (see Appendix A).

The following scenarios are examples of bad landlord behaviour:

- Evicting you for no good reason
- Shutting off your heat or reducing it to an unreasonably low temperature
- Entering your rented space without giving twenty-four hours' notice (okay only in cases of emergency)
- Not repairing plumbing problems
- Not helping you address insect or rodent issues when you report them to the landlord
- Changing the lock and not giving you the new keys
- Not giving your security deposit back to you
- Not letting you sublet the apartment to a new, credible tenant

Nine years ago, I found an apartment above a bakery. I thought this place was a dream! For $1,000 a month I actually landed a 3-bedroom apartment that had a large living room, a 150-foot rooftop patio, and I could even make noise there, which was important because I was a musician. Now on the surface, I'm sure it sounds like I won the apartment lottery, but over time I grew to absolutely loathe—and I emphasize the word loathe—that place.

My apartment was on a busy road that led drivers to one of the important urban highways, so, besides the constant movement and basic traffic noise, there would be people honking their car horns every 3-5 minutes (probably notifying some idiot that the light had changed and it was time to drive already)! As well, the street was a city bus route that ran a 24-hour service so if I wanted to have my window open I'd be sucking in bus exhaust fumes from my bedroom window. Right across the street from me there was also a questionable bar-type establishment, so on a fairly regular basis there would be the "been through a lot" types spilling out onto the street, drunk and engaging in fights. The general "vibe" of the neighbourhood was not so great, so it was not unusual to have questionable characters around. For example, my front door ended up with at least seven different graffiti tags on it, and my landlord did not do anything about it.

Now that just gives you an idea about the outside of my apartment – as for the inside, there were so many issues I had to face that I could go on for hours without making a single thing up!

As I mentioned, I was on the second floor, above the bakery that my landlord owned and operated. He had an industrial-sized air conditioner that ran 24 hours a day to cool the bakery. Maybe there was something wrong with it, or maybe that's just how these machines operate, but basically after its 15 seconds of normal deafening noise it would have rolling 3-second intervals of a low growling sound that was totally audible for about sixty percent of the day, to me and to all the surrounding neighbours. The bad thing was that it did not even cool my place whatsoever. My apartment was a total inferno because I was on the top floor of the building, so the heat from the sun beat down on the roof and the heat from the bakery below rose up to my apartment!

Not only were there problems with overheating, in the winter my heat never worked—it was totally freezing in there. My landlord's advice was to open the radiators, but I opened them often and it did absolutely nothing, so I spent most winters wearing several layers of sweaters. He was just too cheap to fix it.

Because there was a bakery downstairs I also ended up seeing a small number of cockroaches from time to time. I told my landlord, but his response was: "They're not going to kill you, ha ha ha!" So, basically I bought this Borax powder and heavily laced my apartment with it to the point that it looked like I was walking around on flour. God knows what kind of health effect that had on me, but I suppose in the end the landlord was right—neither the cockroaches nor the Borax killed me . . .

Every time something was wrong, it was almost impossible to get a hold of the landlord. He didn't have e-mail and he also didn't have voice mail, so if he didn't want to pick up the phone, it would just ring and ring and ring. If I wanted to get anything fixed, I had to go to the bakery and ask the people at the counter if he was in. Sometimes they would just say I don't know and they would walk to the back to see if the landlord would come to see me or not. Sometimes I'd have to stand there and wait and wait and wait just in case he would actually come out and talk to me.

One day when I came back from a trip, I was woken up at three a.m. by the sound of my carbon monoxide alarm. I called the fire department and they discovered unhealthy levels of CO in my *apartment, coming from the bakery and seeping through my floor boards. But no one in the business would answer the door, so they issued the CO notice to me to give to the landlord. I told them the landlord would not take it seriously unless the fire department delivered it personally, but they simply couldn't get anyone to answer the door. Two months later the alarm went off again and I called the fire department again—this time they managed to get into the bakery and discovered near-fatal levels of CO, so they shut down the business for a day.*

Because it was a bakery, people were working in the shop fairly long hours (it opened every day at 4:30 a.m.) and so from 10 a.m. to 10 p.m., seven days a week, they would play this Portuguese radio station. Of course, the apartment was such that the sound from this radio would bleed up into my place. I'd have to listen to this constant droning sound of mumbling Portuguese and, if you can't imagine it, I can attest that this was totally frustrating, annoying, and unpleasant. When I went downstairs to see where the sound was coming from, I noticed that the speakers were pointed upwards towards the ceiling (my apartment floor) and away from the customers at the bakery! I asked them to turn the speakers away but they didn't change it, so I started to avoid my apartment, staying at my parents' place and with friends, only dropping by to pick things up. I spent months doing this, while still paying full rent. This issue was really the ultimate straw for me. Basically I told him that if he didn't stop playing this radio station I was going to take the issue to the City to get it resolved through the landlord and tenant dispute resolution services. It was actually the only time he responded to my complaint.

Finally, I just decided to get out of there. I threw out half my stuff, stored the rest in my parents' place, and left to spend some time in other cities. I figured that sometimes you just have to jump into the water and allow yourself an opportunity to make connections to other places and people. I've decided that, in the future, any place I live in doesn't have to be big—it will just have to be in a pleasant environment in a neighbourhood that I would enjoy living in.

Rodrigo
Hamilton, Ontario

I found a roommate through an ad on my university bulletin board. I shared a two-bedroom apartment on one floor of a house with another female university student. She signed the one-year lease on behalf of both of us. She was totally responsible, and we were both able to pay our rent on time. She was quiet and had a high standard in terms of keeping our apartment clean. Sometimes she had to "remind me" that it was my turn to clean the bathroom or the kitchen, which was maybe irresponsible on my part, but I was super-busy juggling full-time university, a part-time job, and a social life. I also just didn't really care about being as clean and tidy as she was. Overall, it was a good experience (at least for me)! We both had to move out when the landlord put his house up for sale and he found a buyer who did not want any tenants.

Sarah, Calgary, Alberta

Evictions from the Apartment

Eviction is when a landlord forces a tenant to move out. A tenant can be evicted for any number of reasons, such as:

- The tenant is not paying the rent in full or at all
- The tenant fails to make payments on the date the rent is due
- The tenant is excessively and unreasonably noisy
- The tenant has damaged the property beyond normal wear and tear
- The tenant is engaging in illegal activity on the premises (e.g., selling drugs)
- The tenant is caught smoking in a non-smoking apartment unit
- The tenant is caught housing a pet in an apartment where no pets are allowed
- The tenant is caught barbequing on the balcony when it is not allowed
- The landlord sells the house and the new owners do not want to have tenants
- The landlord has to make significant renovations that cannot be done while the tenant is residing there
- The landlord wishes to regain the property as his/her own family dwelling
- The landlord becomes bankrupt and loses the house

In some provinces and territories, like Ontario, you actually do not have to move out if your landlord just tells you that you are evicted from the apartment because of something you've done. If you don't actually want to leave the apartment, you have a right to appear at a hearing to state your case. The board can decide who is in the right (you or the landlord). Tenant rights are set by each province or territory, so they vary across Canada. Consult Appendix A of this book (Residential Tenancy Dispute Resolution Services and Information) to identify the appropriate department or board you should contact for more information.

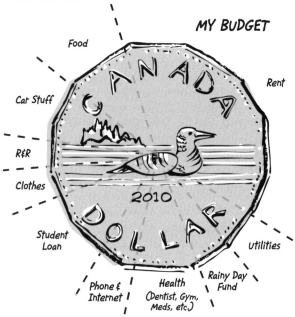

MY BUDGET

Food

Rent

Car Stuff

R&R

Clothes

Student Loan

Utilities

Phone & Internet

Health (Dentist, Gym, Meds, etc.)

Rainy Day Fund

 # The Cost of Living on Your Own

*L*iving on your own is expensive because you pay 100 percent of all costs, including rent, hydro (electricity), utilities (e.g., natural gas), cable, landline telephone, the car, car insurance and parking (if applicable), food, cleaning costs, furniture purchasing, gardening (if applicable), pets (if applicable), etc. While few people like to develop a budget, it can help you determine if you can afford to live independently within your current income level.

Budget Sample
— Monthly Living Costs That Suit Your Budget

As an example, you could try developing your own budget forecast like this:

Monthly Income	$2,000
Minus	
Rent	$850 (add anticipated hydro or utilities, if separate)
Phone/Internet/Cable TV*	$125
Food and sundries	$450 (food, deodorant, laundry soap, light bulbs, etc.)
Transit	$160 (public transit, taxis, parking)
Laundry	$35 (increase the amount if you need dry cleaning)
Clothes, extras	$90 (e.g., shirts, shoe repair, music buying)
Entertainment	$75 (may include eating out)
Banking fees	$15 (monthly bank charge, ATM and point of sale charge)
Other	$100 (buffer for irregular expenses, like gifts, haircuts, etc.)
Savings / debt payment	$100 (moving fund, RRSP investment, debt payment)
Total Expenses	**$2,000 (balance expenses to match your income)**

* These days more people are choosing not to pay cable television fees. Many shows can be watched free of charge on the Internet at www.casttv.com.

This budget sample assumes that you don't own a car and aren't paying apartment insurance. You can modify your budget costs and amounts to suit your own personal situation. Just make sure the budget expenses balance to match your income. Always factor in some buffer room for "other" expenses, because unanticipated costs are inevitably going to pop up.

The second time I moved, I lived in a semi-detached house with three other girls. One of them had been someone I knew from the university residence. Another girl was someone I had met twice before and the last girl was a friend-of-a-friend. We had to sign a one-year lease and we also had to pay our hydro (electricity) bill on top of the cost of the rent. One of the other girls signed up for the hydro bill. When she got the bill, she sent all of us a message on Facebook to tell us how much we each owed. It was really expensive to pay that bill every two months—especially in the winter. Those bills were about $200 for each of us! We had baseboard heating, which I've heard is the most expensive kind. We tried our best to keep electricity costs low. We agreed to limit the number of showers each of us had every week and limited the duration (to reduce hot water usage). We also did our laundry using the "cold" cycle. One girl always had her boyfriend over and we didn't like the feeling that we were probably paying for him to be a fifth person taking showers. One girl decided that she preferred to do her laundry with warm water, which was annoying.

When we first moved in together, we were in a kind of "honeymoon" roommate phase where it was all fun, everyone was easygoing and nice, and we generally ate together and watched reality TV shows together. But the constant undercurrent of little nagging tensions put a bit of a damper on things. We were not very good at communicating directly with each other about what was bothering us. For example, the house was always so dirty but no one wanted to ask anyone else to clean up her mess.

Anyway, all in all it was not so bad. It's summer so I'm back at home for now. I look forward to my next apartment when school starts back up in the fall because the three people who live there state their expectations and general house rules up front. It's clear.

Heather
Ottawa, Ontario

My roommates and I lived on the third floor of a commercial/ residential building. Floors one and two were rented by an IT company, so our landlord gave us free Internet access. Since we were students, we went to town streaming and downloading TV *shows, movies, and songs. By the third month, the landlord came and told us that he noticed he was eighty gigabytes over his limit. I don't know what kind of plan he had with his company, but when you go over your plan the company charges something like five to ten dollars per extra gigabyte used. Unfortunately, the landlord cut off our free Internet at that point. We then had to factor Internet payments into our monthly budgets.*

Jeff, Kingston, Ontario

Apartment Content Insurance

Some people like to buy apartment content insurance. This insurance, paid monthly, can be purchased through a bank or insurance company to cover the estimated cost of replacing the contents of your apartment in the case of fire or other damage. You might want to insure your furniture, art work, musical instruments, entertainment equipment, etc. You may need to take photos of everything for proof. Apartment insurance costs can be negotiated or reduced if it is bundled in with your car insurance (if applicable). Consider whether your stuff really needs to be insured or not. Weigh the monthly insurance cost (consider how much it will cost you to insure your things for a whole year) versus the real value of your items. Ask yourself if paying the monthly fee is really worth it to you.

 **Roommates**

MANY PEOPLE TRY LIVING WITH ROOMMATES TO COST-SHARE. This can be practical and fun because you might end up with an excellent support system if you buddy up with a friend or two (emotional support and sharing clothes, food, furniture, cable/Internet cost, etc.). You might even take a chance and buddy up with roommates you don't know because the apartment you want is in a neighbourhood or price range you're interested in. Check out *www.ca/easyroommate.com* to research potential roommate options. It's got photos and brief personal descriptions of potential roommates as well as apartment photos.

WHILE LIVING WITH A ROOMMATE CAN HAVE MANY POSITIVES, IT CAN ALSO PRESENT ITS OWN SET OF CHALLENGES because people have different habits, expectations, and beliefs and because strangers (if you're not bunking with friends) rarely have any fundamental reason to care about you or to be loyal to you. If you choose to live with a roommate, learning to communicate diplomatically is a good skill, as well as learning the patience of give and take. Sometimes you'll need to cut your roommate some slack and sometimes they'll need to give you a break as well.

HAVE A SERIOUS CONVERSATION WITH A POTENTIAL ROOMMATE BEFORE MOVING IN TOGETHER, TO TRY AND FIGURE OUT SOME OF THE "WHAT-IF" SCENARIOS:

- What if one of you wants to move somewhere else?
- What will each of you do if you hit a hard economic time — how will your/their rent be paid?
- What are your rules about overnight guests and noise at night?
- How long is it okay to leave the dishes in the sink?
- Who cleans the fridge and the bathroom, and what's the schedule?

Does the potential roommate you're talking to sound responsible? Does he/she have a good head on his/her shoulders, seem free of serious problems and addictions? Although some of those things sound petty, they are often the cause of arguments and bad vibes at home. Who needs that?

I moved out on my own when I finished high school. Two of my close high school friends agreed to live with me in a four-bedroom apartment downtown. We got a fourth lady to join us, but it didn't work out. She would leave her dirty laundry in random places like the living room and she'd never wash her dishes, especially when she went away for the weekend. Finally we couldn't take it any more. We gave her a letter saying we wanted her out. She packed up and left but not before damaging a piece of our furniture and stealing our stereo. Still, we considered it a good tradeoff not to have to deal with her any more!

Véronique, Ottawa, Ontario

On one of my moves I decided to live with my brother. He and his fiancée signed the lease. It got awkward when the two of them broke up and she decided to still live there with us. She was kind of a slob and she had boxes of her stuff in common areas. At some point, the three of us decided to get a puppy together and to share the responsibility. We all agreed to take turns walking the dog and to share the costs. In the first month it was going really well and I fell in love with that puppy. One day I came home to find out that this girl had packed up our puppy and taken him away to a shelter, stating that she had "allergies." There was no group discussion about it—she just decided. I was really upset but there was nothing I could do.

At this place, there was only one real parking spot. Both my brother and I had cars. We decided to park one car behind the other in the driveway. That year I learned how to park within an inch of another car. We decided that whoever had to leave first the next morning would take whichever car was parked in the outside spot. My brother got the best deal, since he had a beater car with no air conditioning or heat. Can't say I never did anything for him!

Elizabeth
Windsor, Ontario

My boyfriend and I rented a two-bedroom apartment in downtown Vancouver. We fell into a bit of financial hard times so we needed to look for a roommate to help offset the costs. We placed an ad in the neighbourhood newspaper and found a young woman who seemed kind of edgy and cool. We liked that about her because I was an artist and my boyfriend was a musician. Anyway, we soon found out that she was not altogether stable. She seemed to have some kind of an eating disorder because all she ever ate were rice cakes. One day we came home and found her crashed out on the sofa. She had tried to commit suicide by overdose. We got her into my car, took the pill bottle, and drove her to the hospital, where they pumped her stomach. Luckily she survived. She had to stay there for observation for twenty-four hours. She came back home and continued living with us. My boyfriend and I were as supportive as we could be but *we were kind of scared that she was going to try it again. She left us when her boyfriend proposed to marry her and they went off to live together. Not to be mean or anything, but we were kind of relieved.*

Adam and Vanessa
Vancouver, British Columbia

My girlfriend and I moved into a fairly expensive two-bedroom apartment because it was conveniently located close to work and we liked the neighbourhood. We agreed that we would get a roommate so we posted an ad on-line. I got a call from a mother whose son was dating a girl. I told her that we were only looking for one roommate, not two. I thought that I was clear but the next day I came home from work and I found that guy and his girlfriend sitting in my living room talking to my girlfriend. For some reason, my girlfriend ended up liking them and she thought we could make it work. So although I thought it would be a mistake to take two people instead of one, I agreed. They shared a bedroom and we all shared the bathroom, living room, and kitchen.

Sometimes we took turns cooking for the other couple and vice-versa. I hated it when the girl had seriously little awareness of others. If I was cooking, sometimes she would just come right in and take over. Other times I would be watching TV, and she would have her own loud phone conversations in there regardless of what I was doing. One time her parents showed up and parked their camper van outside. Without any discussion with us, she told her cousins that they could sleep on the floor in our living room. After three months of this kind of behaviour, I had had it with them. I'm not a very religious guy but I put my hands together and I prayed hard for something to happen so we could get them out. Astonishingly, the very next day the boyfriend broke up with this girl and he moved out. The broken-hearted girl listened to Coldplay incessantly for two weeks straight, which was totally annoying, but then she finally moved out. I am still amazed to this day by the power of prayer!

Don and Tina
Regina, Saskatchewan

 **Moving Out**

Moving Costs

There is quite a significant cost to moving. These costs can include:

- Preparing to pay first and last month's rent up front at the beginning

- Hiring movers

- Buying boxes, packing tape, and packing paper

- Providing a meal for friends or family who are helping you move

- Van or truck rental if you are moving yourself

- Phone, Internet, and cable hookup fees in your new place

- Buying new furniture or home supplies

- Paying for a temporary Canada Post mail forwarding service (six months or one year)

Moving Dates

- A few people move on the first day of the month.
- Some people move on the 15th day of the month.
- Most people typically move on the last day of the month.
- Sometimes a space will come available in the last few days of the month so you may be able to move in a few days before the end of the month.

Movers: Your Friends and Family

The best movers are usually friends and family. When they help you move, consider them as your angel helpers, because moving is hard work — it's a lot of lifting, and the experience is usually aggravated by stairs and doors that seem particularly small when you're holding heavy or awkward-shaped things. Make sure you feed your movers and give them beverages — especially water! Although it's hard to stop and take breaks while moving, it is easy to get dehydrated. Take short beverage breaks now and then!

My best friend and I decided to get an apartment together. We agreed to help each other with the moving instead of paying professional movers. My friend kind of had a lot of stuff, so we rented a U-Haul truck. That truck was so hard to drive because a) it didn't have power steering; b) it was really hard to see around the back of the truck using those mirrors; and c) the vehicle was in general really large and wide compared to the compact car I was used to driving.

Anyway, we managed moving his stuff better than mine, because I borrowed a friend's pickup truck to move my rackety student furniture. I put my stuff in the back, and we did our best to tie it down. We figured it was fine; he was an engineering student, so that gave me extra confidence that it was okay. We started driving on the highway and noticed the back of my Ikea bookshelf flying off the truck, and the base of my chair was starting to fly off as well! We quickly pulled over to the side of the highway. Luckily no one was directly behind us at that moment! I ran back to get the piece of my bookshelf, and we put my stuff back in and tried our best to re-tie everything down. If I can give anyone advice about moving stuff with a pickup truck it's this: use a tarp, people!

Finally, we did manage to make it to our destination without any other trouble. We had rented a two-bedroom apartment in a small apartment building with six units. Although we signed a one-year lease, our landlord, who was also a resident there, threatened to kick us out so many times because he thought we were too loud. One of our friends used to just show up and hang out with us, and occasionally we had other friends over—like the time we had a wine and cheese gathering at our place during the ice storm, and the landlord freaked out about it. I swear we weren't being party animals—the walls were just paper thin. You could absolutely hear everything in the neighbours' apartments. Our landlord did not even like us watching television and he told us he thought we should buy headsets for our TV, which is what he did. In our view, that was totally ridiculous. In the end, our landlord agreed to just let us break the lease and move out of there when the school year was over. I was glad to not have to worry anymore whether idiotic stuff like the clang of dishes when I put them away was too much for the "decibel cop."

Anthony
Montreal, Quebec

Movers: The Professionals

Selecting the best professional moving company can be tricky. If you don't have family or friends to help you, or if you feel you've asked them to help you move too many times, it's time to call the professionals, and it's going to cost you a fair bit of money.

WHERE TO FIND A GOOD MOVING COMPANY
- Visit the Canadian Association of Movers on the Internet for a list of reliable movers in your city.
- Ask friends who have moved recently for references.
- Call up a bunch of movers in the Yellow Pages of the telephone book to ask for a "moving quote" that will give you an estimate on the price and the amount of time they think it will take them

to move you. Contact at least three companies so that you'll get a sense of an average price. As well, sometimes movers will ask you different questions. Speaking to a variety of professionals will ensure that you've covered the basic parameters of the services you'll need and give you confidence that you are hiring the best company for your requirements and budget.

- Once you have a moving company in mind, you might want to check if they are members of the Better Business Bureau in your city, which can increase your confidence in their credibility as a good, reliable company.

DETERMINING MOVING COST PRICES

An estimate of time is part of what a mover considers in quoting you a price. Find out on MapQuest Driving Directions the distance and length of time it's going to take you from your current location to your new location. Consider how much stuff you have. Movers will judge the time they'll need based on the type of apartment you have (bachelor, one-bedroom, two-bedroom) and any pieces of big furniture you might have (bed, couch, desk, dresser, washer and dryer, table, etc.).

SIGNING A MOVING AGREEMENT

Many movers will ask you to sign a Moving Agreement form (or contract) when they arrive at your place. It should at the very least outline the price of the job. Beware: in rare cases there have been recent scams in Ontario whereby the mover will tell you one price, load up your belongings in his truck, and then state that he will not drive you to your new location until you pay more, due to some tiny fine print in a "contractual moving agreement" or "company policy." In this case, the provincial government is supporting consumers and they advise that you call the police immediately if you are faced with this type of extortion threat.

Weigh issues of price and number of movers you'll need to help you and consider whether you want to ask for boxing services or if you want to box all your things up yourself. Most people just box their stuff themselves because it's cheaper and because they have a sense of how they want their stuff to be packed.

Moving boxes can be purchased at certain times of the year at "big box" stores like Wal-Mart (usually only in the summer months); or from rental storage space companies and moving companies at any time; or, in some cities, from *www.movingboxes.ca*. If you know someone working in an office building, he/she can watch for suitable boxes for you as well (e.g., boxes from paper packages, which usually have good handles). Otherwise, some grocery stores have boxes you can take for free, but not all stores will let you have them, so it takes some planning. It is also helpful to buy actual plastic boxes at a store like Loblaws or Wal-Mart. It's nice because they are sturdy, stack well, and can be reused the next time you move; or they can be used for storage if you do not have enough closet space.

Special Moving Tips

* *Consider saving money to build up a moving fund for yourself.* When everything is added up — from moving supplies, movers, phone/cable activation, first and last month's rent, etc. — moving usually costs several hundred dollars; but most likely you will be looking at needing well over a thousand dollars to set yourself up properly.

* *Try to book your moving company as far in advance as you possibly can.* Competition to get a mover on the day you want can be high (since most people move on the last day of the month, that's a lot of concentrated demand).

* *Invest in Canada Post's temporary mail-forward service.* Consider buying a temporary mail-forward service from Canada Post for a six-month or one-year period. This way, for a small fee you can make sure that any organization or company you forgot to notify about your new address can still reach you. When you get forwarded mail, contact the company/organization immediately with your new residential mail and telephone information.

* *Reserve a date for telephone/Internet/cable TV installation.* As soon as you have your new address and moving date, arrange for telephone and cable set-up in advance. Sometimes it can take up to a couple of weeks for the company to give you an appointment. Weekend times are especially hard to get. If you don't book in advance, it might be an extraordinarily long time

until the next free weekend. They may only give you a weekday time, which might mean that you'll have to take time off work or school. Figure out in advance if you want more than one telephone jack (e.g., a phone in the living room and one in the bedroom).

- *Get rid of things you don't use.* We accumulate a lot of "stuff." Pare it down. Get rid of things you don't actually need or use. It will make packing and moving a lot easier. For example, try advertising things on a Web site that lists used items for sale (e.g., *www.kijiji.ca*), if your items good enough. Or, put any unwanted books in a box out on the lawn or in the lobby with a sign that says "FREE." Put other furniture you don't want there as well. If they're not broken, they'll get picked up. Consider donating things to the Goodwill, Salvation Army, or Value Village. Making donations to women's or men's shelters can be an excellent option as well. Call the shelter first. They usually have a particular day in the week for you to drop off your items. Consider making a donation to visual artists, who usually need old clothing to use as rags to clean their paintbrushes.

- *Buy some inexpensive, good-quality home furnishings.* Buy some things second hand. Check out Web sites that advertise used items for sale. Sometimes people have to move quickly and they actually get rid of a lot of really good stuff. You can often buy things you need very inexpensively that way. To ensure your own personal security, go to strangers' places with a friend when you buy items.

- *Invest in your own packing tape dispenser.* This is an extremely handy tool. It lasts forever.

- *Purchase other packing tools.* Complementary packing tools include rolls of packing tape, packing paper and/or bubble wrap to protect breakables (can be purchased from storage facilities and some big box stores), and an industrial-quality exacto knife (stronger than the little arts and crafts type).

- *Support your packing boxes.* Make sure your packing boxes are well supported on the inside bottom of the box (reinforced with packing tape).

- *Don't make your boxes too heavy.* They'll be hard to lift and may break, causing you major frustration and costing you extra time and materials to repack!

- *Label your boxes.* Use an easily legible marker or label, listing the contents of the box (this way you'll know what's in each box and can find stuff quickly) and, more important, the room it should be placed in once moved. This way you get more mileage out of your movers — they can carry and place your boxes in the appropriate room (bathroom, kitchen, living room, bedroom, etc.).

- *Supervise your movers.* This tip is especially important when you are paying movers to help you. Sometimes your possessions are not the only items in their moving truck. It is ultimately up to you to ensure that all of your boxes make it onto the moving truck or van and that all of them make it off the vehicle and into your new home.

- *Be courteous to the next tenant.* When you move, it is especially polite and thoughtful if you can factor in some time before you go to clean your place for the next tenant. This will mean that the last things you pack are the cleaning supplies and tools (e.g., broom and dustpan, cleaning cloths, and soap). In some provinces, such as Manitoba, the landlord will actually keep your security deposit if you haven't cleaned the place to his/her satisfaction on vacating the premises.

- *Leave on good terms.* Remember that the best scenario is when you can leave your apartment on good terms with your landlord, because he or she may be called in the future as a reference to reassure a new prospective landlord that you are a good tenant.

PACKING TAKES WAY LONGER THAN YOU EXPECT! You will not believe how much time packing takes and how exhausting it is. You absolutely must be ready with everything packed by the time your paid professional movers or your friends/family arrive to help you load up your belongings and move to the next place. There's nothing worse than paying professionals for their time while they are waiting for you to finish packing; or making friends or family mad that their precious time is being wasted on one of the hardest jobs ever — packing and moving!

Whom to Inform When You Move

- Your friends and family

- Your workplace

- If you are age eighteen or older: Canada Revenue Agency (this ensures that you get your voter registration card in the next election)

- If you are on Social Assistance (i.e., welfare): your provincial or territorial government

- Ministry of Health (for your health card — see Appendix B)

- Ministry of Transportation (your driver's licence)

- Car/apartment insurance company

- Your bank

- Any firm where you have investments (like an RRSP, mutual funds, or savings bonds)

- All your bill payment companies (landline telephone, mobile phone, cable, hydro, car loan or lease, car/apartment content insurance, any non-bank credit cards, etc.)

- Your union, if your workplace has representation

- Your gym

- Your company/government health insurance plan

- College/university or alumni association

- Any clubs or associations you belong to

- Doctor

- Dentist

- Store club cards / points cards you care about

- Video store

- Any store where you are selling items on consignment

Household Items You'll Need

While it is nice having new things, it is surprising how many items can be purchased in excellent condition second-hand; check out Web sites that list used items for sale, like Kijiji. Dollar stores can be a great place to find inexpensive basic home items (canned goods, cleaning supplies, kitchenware, etc.). Hand-me-downs from friends and family or great finds at garage sales are often an excellent way to score what you need as well!

Consider taking this book with you when you go shopping for supplies. Mark off the bullets to help you track your purchases and complete your home supplies. If you're moving in with roommates, check to see what they have first so you don't buy things you don't need.

Kitchen[2]

- ❏ Pots and pans, baking sheet, baking pot
- ❏ Dishes (plates, bowls, glasses, mugs, serving bowls)
- ❏ Silverware and serving spoons
- ❏ Placemats
- ❏ Dishcloths (like thin face cloths) to wash the dishes (they are better than disposable J-cloths or sponges for washing the dishes. They can be put in the washing machine and used for a very long time, which reduces unnecessary garbage)
- ❏ Dish towels
- ❏ Enviro-degradable soap
- ❏ Glass containers for food storage (preferable to plastic)
- ❏ Salt and pepper shakers
- ❏ Spice/herb jars
- ❏ Garlic press
- ❏ Spatula
- ❏ Cutting knives
- ❏ Cutting board
- ❏ Dish drainer

---

2   Note: In Quebec, it is sometimes a requirement that you supply your own fridge and stove when renting an apartment. Ask the landlord. If you go and view the apartment and you see a fridge and stove, they might actually belong to the tenant. If so, you could negotiate with the tenant to purchase these items to save both of you the hassle of buying and moving major appliances.

- ❑ Strainer
- ❑ Coffee maker / teapot
- ❑ Sugar bowl
- ❑ Microwave
- ❑ Toaster
- ❑ Blender / food processor
- ❑ Coasters to avoid those nasty ring stains on furniture
- ❑ Trivets to place your hot pots/ bowls onto
- ❑ Fridge magnets
- ❑ Oven mitts
- ❑ Kitchen table
- ❑ Chairs
- ❑ Vase
- ❑ Garbage can
- ❑ Recycling containers
- ❑ Multi-purpose, dry chemical fire extinguisher

Bedroom

- ❑ Bed
- ❑ Sheets
- ❑ Blankets
- ❑ Pillows
- ❑ Dresser
- ❑ Hangers
- ❑ Laundry hamper
- ❑ Desk
- ❑ Chair
- ❑ Mirror
- ❑ Lamps
- ❑ Nightstand
- ❑ Alarm clock
- ❑ Trash can

Living Room

- ❑ Couch
- ❑ End table(s) or centre table
- ❑ Chairs
- ❑ Carpet
- ❑ Lamps
- ❑ Television and television stand
- ❑ DVD player and/or Personal Video Recorder (PVR)
- ❑ Radio / sound system
- ❑ Bookcase
- ❑ Art work, posters, picture frames

Bathroom

- ❑ Bath towels
- ❑ Hand towels for guests
- ❑ Face cloths
- ❑ Towel rack
- ❑ Bath mat
- ❑ Essential oil room spray (health food store)
- ❑ Toilet plunger
- ❑ Squeegee to remove excess water from the shower walls (to reduce humidity and mould)
- ❑ Trash can with closing lid

General Cleaning Materials and Supplies

- Vacuum cleaner
- Broom and dustpan
- Duster
- Wet cleaning tool for uncarpeted floors
- Bathroom and kitchen cleaning products. (Try to purchase green/eco products to avoid bringing nasty chemicals into your home. Many cleaning supplies can present this problem.)

Other Necessary Items

- Phone(s) (e.g., in the living room and bedroom)
- Phone books (both personal and city)
- Iron
- Ironing board
- Spray bottle for ironing
- Coat rack
- Mirror by the front door for that final check!
- Shoe rack at the front door
- Interior doormat (for wiping off dirt and snow)
- Slippers for you and extra pairs for visitors to your home (super cheap in Chinatown!)
- Smoke detector / fire alarm outside the bedroom door and on every floor of the residence
- Carbon monoxide detector
- Cross-cutter document shredder
- Flashlight, candles, and matches (the electricity will likely go out during a storm at some point)
- Humidifier (great to hydrate your space during the super-dry Canadian winter months)
- Dehumidifier (especially helpful to get rid of the dampness in basement apartments)
- Snow shovel (if you are responsible for clearing the walk)
- Salt or sand for icy sidewalks and stairs in winter
- Accordion folder to file your bills, receipts, tax papers
- Home exercise equipment and exercise DVDs
- Home alarm system if you feel it is necessary
- Spare light bulbs in the wattage you need

❏ Hammer, nails, multi-head screwdriver, picture frame hooks of various weight tolerances

❏ Charger and rechargeable batteries

❏ Basic sewing kit (basic thread colours, needles, scissors, safety pins, seam ripper)

❏ Packing tape and packing tape dispenser

❏ Packing paper / bubble wrap to protect breakables

❏ Cloth fruit and vegetable produce bags (e.g., as found on *www.carebagsonline. com*) — they're made from 100-percent recycled material and they're made in Canada!

❏ Plants

❏ Computer

❏ Printer

Although I was born in Canada, my parents moved the family back to India after my dad completed his Ph.D. at the University of British Columbia and had put in a few years of research and academics. We were very fortunate to visit Canada many times while I was growing up. Two decades later, my brother moved to Canada to study medicine and he got married here. When I finished my Masters degree in India, I got my first job and I bought my mom two sarees with my very first paycheque. My mom helped me develop some financial management skills by taking me to the bank to open my very first bank account, get an ATM card, and order some cheques. And she taught me how to save. Over the course of that year, my mom encouraged me to go and live in Canada. So when I was twenty-four I left home, travelled from India to Toronto with just two suitcases of clothing, books, and jewellery, and moved in with my brother and his new wife. I lived with them for a few months while I applied for jobs.

Thankfully I won a federal government job in Winnipeg, so my extended family graciously allowed me to move into a self-contained apartment suite in their home. Besides learning things like how to dress for the shocking reality of a Canadian winter (e.g., woollen socks, long johns, and real winter gloves were a definite must-have!), it was here that I took small steps to develop an ability to live on my own. In all my life I had never, ever once eaten a meal alone because it was not our cultural way, but Winnipeg is where I learned how to shop for groceries, cook for myself and, although my extended family and I ate together sometimes, I managed to learn that it was okay to eat alone. Watching TV helped because it gave me some other noise and activity to keep me occupied.

By the spring I decided I wanted my own place. I looked in the classified ads in the newspaper for an apartment, but my brother encouraged me to buy a house because houses weren't very expensive in Winnipeg at the time. A friend of the family was a real estate agent and she showed me several options. I knew very clearly what I liked and what I didn't like. Finally, I found a little place that was just right, and my brother helped me with the down payment. Then, I had to register with companies for my phone, television, hydro, etc. and I had to buy every single thing to make a home livable. I bought kitchenware, sheets, a bed, a couch, a TV, bathroom towels — you name it, I needed it! Once my home was complete, I had a huge sense of fulfillment. I was able to have my mom, my brother, and my friends over whenever I wanted to. I have since moved to Ottawa and overall I am very grateful to live in Canada. It is so beautiful here. I just got home from a trip to Algonquin Park, which was spectacular!

Sujata
Ottawa, Ontario

PHONE BOOK

Even though everything is getting digitized these days and most numbers are captured in a phone, you may still want to keep an old-fashioned paper phone book. Sometimes mobile phones get lost or stolen or they just die — then it's really going to be a pain if you lose all your contacts. If you do get yourself a paper phone book, think about choosing a small, slim one you can carry around if you need to. I especially strongly recommend writing down all names and numbers in pencil. People move fairly frequently or stores go out of business, or you move. Pencil is a good option because it's annoying and ugly to have to use liquid paper to remove entries or to have to restart a new phone book.

It's also super handy to record numbers from places you frequent a fair bit. This will help you avoid 411 charges when it's getting late, you're feeling lazy, can't find a phone book, or whatever, and you'd just prefer to incur the charge.

Phone numbers I generally keep are:

- Under D: Drugstore and hours. This is especially handy when you're sick and you're alone and you have to drag yourself out and get supplies.

- L: Landlord

- M: Medical for your doctor or walk-in medical clinics. Or the Mall — note the mall hours and any particular store phone numbers in the mall that you like. Under M I also write Member of Parliament. This number is handy if there's a political or a social issue you hope your Member will address or resolve; or it's handy if you have a question about voter registration or voting location.

- T (for taxes): the Canada Revenue Agency

- W: I usually write down the numbers of people at work, including managers, co-workers, and tech support. These numbers are especially important when you have to call in sick or if you're running late. Communicating this info to your manager in a timely manner can show that you care, which is important for maintaining a good reputation and for reminding them that you are responsible.

There are probably other numbers you might want to think about adding to your book. "V" for vet; "C" for car or CAA; and so on.

Emergency contacts are good to note in your phone book so that family and friends can be contacted in case of emergency to speak for you when you can't speak for yourself. As a related element, it has become fairly standard to note emergency contacts in your mobile phone under ICE1, ICE2 (In Case of Emergency), for a situation in which you are incapacitated, and helpers will need to know whom to call.

The Practice of "Everything in Its Place"

When you live alone, you may wish you could call out to someone to help you find that thing you just can't find, but you might as well be yelling into a canyon at sunset! Best strategy is to find a permanent storage place for all your stuff by assigning a specific place for everything. Your keys should have their own place. So should your cell phone, your camera, your recharging devices, your mail, your slippers, your jewellery, your hair elastics, your gym clothes, your scissors, your receipts, your tax papers, etc. Make it easy and fast to find everything. You'll minimize frustration and time-wasting.

The Household Labour

Many people don't talk about the labour of living. They think of labour as related to the workforce. A relatively large degree of labour is required just to take care of yourself and your home day after day, after day, forever. The truth is that home labour is tiring and boring. (You already knew that!)

Most people don't have the luxury to afford a cleaning, cooking, or laundry service. When you live alone, you have to make your home life work day and night, over and over. That's all the cooking and all the cleaning and tidying. There's a lot of it and it's non-stop. Do I have a strategy to deal with this to share with you? No, I don't. Okay, well, playing your favourite music while getting it done sometimes helps. For fun, check out Toronto band Raoul and The Big Time's song, "Movin' Out" on Myspace. In general, you just have to figure out what's an acceptable level of mess or cleanliness for you and try to keep some level of balance. At the very least, when you live on your own the upside is that you don't have to deal with anyone else nagging you about keeping everything clean and tidy, which is a major plus!

 # Health and Well-being

O n a practical level, you will be the most effective person you can be if you commit to taking good care of yourself. When living on your own, no one else is going to help you with this day to day. Sometimes prevention and wellness items, activities, behaviours, and attitudes can include:

- Exercising
- Taking vitamins
- Eating healthy food and having regular meals
- Getting sufficient sleep
- Sleeping in a dark room (darkness enhances quality of sleep)
- Drinking enough water
- Gargling with warm sea-salt water, which kills bacteria
- Washing your hands frequently and avoiding touching your nose
- Brushing and flossing your teeth
- Having a hobby you enjoy
- Grooving to the music you think is cool
- Enjoying the work you do or enjoying what you study
- Volunteering — helping others can make you feel good
- Trusting your instincts or your intuition
- Believing you are good at something, that you are talented, that you have a gift or a specialty, and nurturing it
- Having a pet if you have enough money and time to devote to it and a living space for it
- Dressing appropriately for the weather conditions
- Wearing sun block and sunglasses with ultraviolet light protection
- Getting medical and counselling help for addictions or avoiding excessive alcohol, cigarettes, drugs, and gambling; or joining a support group if you are a family member of someone struggling with addictions
- Getting enough fresh air and sunshine (particularly hard in winter)

- Living within your financial limitations (to avoid financial stress, which can negatively affect health)
- Smiling, laughing, and having an optimistic attitude
- Allowing yourself to be inspired by others
- Finding ways to have fun
- Believing that you are a good person and loving yourself (even if you make mistakes or do wrong things sometimes; like the rest of us, you're learning)
- Finding opportunities to speak your mother tongue (important for languages other than Canada's dominant English language)
- Investing time and effort to improve your English (if it is not your first language) so that you can feel totally comfortable participating fully in society; or, if you are in Quebec, or in some other predominantly francophone community, spend some time improving your French
- Continuing to observe/experience religious or spiritual ceremonies that are a part of your culture if you believe in the power and meaning of them
- Getting an annual medical and dental check-up
- Having the courage to express your feelings to a friend, family member, counsellor, psychologist, or spiritual advisor
- Acknowledging feelings of anger and releasing those feelings safely (such as by speaking calmly to the person who made you angry to try and work it out if you are certain it is safe to do so; exercising; seeking counselling; engaging in law-abiding, peaceful protesting; or through expressing yourself in an artistic medium)
- Having a sense of humour and not taking everything so seriously
- Being courageous enough to live honestly according to your sexual orientation
- If sexually active, asking a new partner about any sexually transmitted disease(s) (STDs) he/she might have or have had, and of course using protection such as condoms, foam, and the pill

- Crying to let stress out (rather than bottling it up)
- Resting when you need to
- Spending time in nature
- Having a creative outlet to express your individuality
- Committing to being a person who enjoys learning (learning whatever!)
- Having the courage to let go of what's not working for you and changing; and exploring or trying something different
- Letting good people into your life
- Nurturing relationships with friends and family you can reach out to for support

Exercise

Let me admit something to you. In general, I have been one of the biggest exercise-haters in the world. When I was a kid I was pretty sporty. As a young adult I just didn't (*get ready for the excuse train . . .*) have the time, the money, the desire, or the willpower. This attitude, coupled with my self-proclaimed "low metabolism" and a desk job, meant that there have been periods when I easily gain weight.

These "fat periods" can really affect your mental and emotional well-being because it is harder to feel good about yourself and harder to have the energy to do things you enjoy. It can also be emotionally more difficult to connect with friends, because being overweight can be an embarrassment. Just realize that fat periods are only "phases," not a life sentence you're stuck with. Just as the body can get fat, it can also get thin.

Having a gym membership can cost a lot, but it can be motivating and convenient. There are a lot of organized sports that can activate your interest and get you moving as well as help you build your friend network. For me, it was falling in love with ballroom dance at the Fred Astaire Dance Studio. I had no clue I would like it until I tried it. For you it might be skiing, sledge hockey, badminton, rock climbing, lacrosse, soccer, swimming, kayaking, volleyball, jogging, walking, yoga, or whatever else. Have some courage to try things and see if they are right for you.

As a practical alternative to a gym membership or joining an organized sport, there are many very effective home DVD workouts that can be inexpensive and can save you a lot of time by cutting down on travelling to and from the gym or club. I'm not getting paid to endorse these videos, so believe me when I tell you that I find the *Ripped* series five-pack DVD set for under forty dollars by Canadian Jari Love to be the most intelligent, easy-to-follow, cool for guys and ladies, and fastest way to lose pounds and reshape your body. I can attest that, as a woman, the super high-repetition weight sets *redefine* your muscles (you don't bulk up — get super-muscular). Jari Love states that a person doesn't bulk up unless you're a guy with lots of testosterone. This weights program apparently raises your metabolism and helps you keep burning calories even post-workout. You can do the video with almost no equipment, although you just might want to buy free weights and a yoga mat (I started out super low, at two to three pounds, while the fit people in the video use five up to twenty-plus pounds). Check out the demos and information at *www.jarilove.com*. Getting in shape is one of the best ways to improve your overall sense of well-being.

Dealing with Illness on Your Own

It is often harder to deal with getting sick when you live alone. Apart from the expense of having to go out and buy supplies all at once when you get sick, it is also a drag to have to physically go out and get the required items to deal with it when you're coughing up a lung, handling a fever, or trying to manage seriously unwelcome stomach troubles. Best thing is to prepare for a variety of needs in advance by building up standard supplies in your medicine cabinet.

Medicine Cabinet Supplies

Some of the Western medical items listed below can be substituted with homeopathic or herbal remedies as well as cheaper generic brands. Be careful to respect your own allergies when purchasing supplies.

- Band-aids

- Polysporin to apply to cuts or minor burns (or a generic brand to pay less)

- Small bottle of rubbing alcohol to disinfect wounds (alcohol never goes bad)

- Thermometer (normal temperature is 35–37 degrees Celsius or approximately 98.6° Fahrenheit; anything higher means you have a fever. A 39°/104° fever is high)

- Ibuprofen or aspirin (instead of a brand name, buy a generic brand to pay less)

- Stomach remedies (heartburn, nausea, diarrhea) (instead of a brand name, buy a generic brand to pay less)

- Cough syrup, cough candies, hot liquid drinks for colds (instead of a brand name, buy a generic brand to pay less)

- Sea salt (for gargling with warm water to kill bacteria in the throat, or to apply on cotton-swab tips to kill bacteria in the nostrils)

- Kleenex

- Cotton-swab tips

- Eye rinse cleaner

- Sun block for UVA and UVB protection

- Topical muscle pain relievers and relaxants (creams or pads)

- Tensors for sprains

- Refreezable ice pack

- First-aid bag that can be heated up in the microwave

- Arnica gel to apply to bruises and sprains

- Hot water bottle

- Cans of soup or dry soup packages (often the food of choice when you have a cold, or are getting back to eating simply after experiencing stomach troubles)

- Condoms to be prepared for sexual health protection

- The pill and Plan B, according to your own reproductive rights point of view (ask the pharmacist)

- Money set aside in an envelope to take a cab to the doctor or walk-in-clinic, emergency room, or to buy medical supplies you don't have. You might want to write down the nearest walk-in clinic addresses, telephone numbers, and hours so you don't have to figure it out when you're sick.

When You're "Sick as a Dog"

Many people have an "I can take it" attitude, but it is important to be prepared to admit that you are actually sicker than a basic something you can deal with at home on your own. When living on your own, you won't have a built-in, second-opinion person living with you to help you determine if a visit to the doctor or emergency room is required. Have the courage to pick up the phone and talk about your symptoms to a friend; or, if you're in Ontario, call Telehealth Ontario 866–797–0000; or call Health Line in Newfoundland & Labrador 888–709–2929 to tell a registered nurse about your symptoms (perhaps other provinces and territories have a similar service that you can find out about by calling your Ministry of Health — see Appendix B). Or just go out and get a professional medical opinion from your doctor, a walk-in clinic, or the hospital emergency room.

Insect and Rodent Elimination

H ere is the section that I didn't want to write about and that nobody likes to talk about. The reality is that if you are a person who moves a fair bit, you are likely going to encounter at least one pest problem at some point. We live in homes and apartments that are safe, warm dwellings that bugs and pests want to get into, particularly to survive our harsh winters and to have ready access to our food and water sources.

Pests are bad. We are not meant to live with them. Pests multiply quickly, and you can soon find yourself overrun by the critters. It is not "cute" if you see a mouse or an ant in your place. For every single individual pest you see, there is likely a large number of their kind nesting and multiplying somewhere that you don't see — so it's best to deal with the problem FAST!

Rodents (mice and rats) and some insects (e.g., cockroaches, ants, silverfish, earwigs, mosquitoes, and flies) carry diseases that can infect us if we get bitten or if we ingest food that they've walked all over. Insects like wasps (which can sting us), cockroaches (which cause us respiratory problems), or bedbugs (which feed off our blood in the night) can actually physically hurt us. Even a moth problem can impact you economically if you have to replace clothes because they're getting "holey" — and I don't mean that in the religious sense of the word! To prevent moths from eating your clothes, you can put cedar wood in your dresser and closet. Cedar blocks can typically be purchased at local hardware stores.

I have personally had to deal with a mouse problem, a fly problem (when I lived next to a farm), an ant problem, and even a bird problem (one got stuck in my fireplace chimney). I am generally one of those "pest-liberator" people, so I always try to address the problems without killing, but sometimes that just doesn't work, and killing the pests is the only realistic option to resolve the problem. Pest control companies often have both lethal and humane/greener options to address problems, if you are a person who is concerned about pesticides and lethal extermination.

The increase in bedbugs is one of the biggest on-the-rise problems facing Canadian cities. If you are planning to move into an apartment building, check the Bedbug Registry at *www.bedbugregistry.com* to see if anyone has reported as a problem the building you're considering. In the "search" box, simply enter in the city and province to pull up all the locations that have been reported to date. To save yourself from being the victim of nasty night-feeders and from the cost of replacing your furniture (such as your mattress, pillows, and couch), avoid renting an apartment in these locations. On this Web site, you can also post your own story, if you've experienced a problem, to warn others. When I typed in, "Vancouver, British Columbia" on the search line, there were 299 postings of bedbug infestation addresses on that date. In Toronto there were 244. In Edmonton there were eleven. Exterminating bedbugs is a lengthy and expensive battle to win. It often requires several treatments by a professional extermination company.

There are things that you can do, as a tenant, to decrease the likelihood of encountering problems such as a cockroach, silverfish, mouse, or rat infestation.

- You need to eliminate food and water sources. Regularly clean your counters, mopping up crumbs and excess water; don't let dishes pile up or soak for too long; clean the inside and behind the fridge and oven/stove; sweep the kitchen floor; vacuum, etc.

- Avoid buying particle-board furniture. The glue is a food source for cockroaches.

- Buy new mattresses, couches, pillows, upholstered chairs, and curtains. Picking these items up from someone's lawn, a garage sale, or buying them second hand can increase the chance that you bring insects and their eggs into your home.

- Avoid renting apartments beside outdoor food markets or above restaurants and grocery stores. These residences have a higher incidence of insect and rodent problems.

- Exterminating some pests is inexpensive and easy, such as buying ant traps at the hardware store. Other pests, such as cockroaches and bedbugs, require a call to a professional extermination company.

- Report any pest issue to your landlord and ask that it be dealt with immediately. If your landlord will not help you, research whether the Landlord and Tenancy Department in your province/ territory (see Appendix A) requires that landlords be responsible to rectify the problem.

- If in the end your landlord does not help you exterminate your pests, hire a pest control company yourself. If you are experiencing an infestation, you may need to treat your furniture and clothing before moving out so as not to bring your infected items to your next residence. Orkin® PCO (*www.orkincanada.ca*) calls itself the largest pest control company in Canada. It has offices in all provinces, but none in the territories.

Your landlord should eliminate all potential pest highways into your place. A landlord should make sure there are no leaky taps and ensure that all cracks and crevices leading into the apartment are caulked and sealed to block unwanted creatures from getting in.

I rented an apartment in a fairly old house. When the season changed and it got cold out, I saw a mouse in my apartment. I didn't want to kill it so I bought a "humane" mousetrap. The trap worked and I caught one. It was a little cage contraption that closed when the mouse went in there and got some food. The next morning, I put the mouse in the trap into my bike bag and I rode it a fair distance to the woods near my workplace, but when I got there, the mouse had already died. I heard after the fact that mice tend to have weak hearts, so it probably had a heart attack. Then, I just seemed to keep seeing more mice. One mouse was huge and it was not afraid of me whatsoever. It liked to engage with me in some kind of a stare-down. I am not making this up: One day that fat mouse somehow managed to get into my fridge and it was in there eating my pizza! I ended up borrowing my landlord's cat, Toby, but it was the dumbest hunter cat ever. All he did was play with the mice. I ended up catching a few more mice and I let them go in a park closer to my house. After about fifteen mice, it came time for me to move out. I never did resolve the problem before I left but I was glad to be through with that experience!

Benoit, Montreal, Quebec

My mom had made me a batch of apple brown sugar muffins, which were wrapped in foil. I left them on the kitchen counter to take with me to school. I started noticing that chunks of the muffin crumble tops were missing and I thought my new roommates may have been picking at them. I didn't want to confront them about it because I didn't want to make waves. In a day or two, I noticed mouse droppings on the counter and realized that it was little critter residents making a meal of my snacks. I told the landlord and he bought some traps for us. My roommate and I used peanut butter on the traps because we heard it was more effective than cheese. We turned off the lights, waited, and presto, those traps killed the mice. Also, since we didn't have any pets to worry about, my landlord put some poison stuff out, too. The poison apparently gets eaten and the chemical dries out the mice so they don't smell as they decompose. I know this is altogether a kind of gross story, but no one needs disease-ridden vermin crawling all over their kitchen. These methods work!

Mike, Toronto, Ontario

 # Finances

Practical Banking Tips

CHEQUES

Everyone needs a chequing account, mostly to pay the rent with cheques or—if you get to that place financially—the mortgage. When you order your cheques, do not ask for your phone number or address to be printed on them—just your name. That way, if you move you don't have to reorder cheques with your new info. You'll save money and hassle. Banks are national. I have lived in other cities or even a different province than the bank where I had opened my account and I found that it actually doesn't matter whatsoever. Just remember the street intersection of your home bank branch (also called "domicile" branch) for security identification when talking to your bank by phone.

OVERDRAFT PROTECTION

A young person might find it smart to pay for a monthly "overdraft protection" service. Overdraft protection is a monthly fee paid to the bank so that the bank will let your cheque go through in those (hopefully) rare moments when you withdraw more money than you actually have in the bank. It is important because you never want your rent cheque to "bounce" — meaning that your landlord gets a notice that you have insufficient funds. If a cheque bounces, there is usually a pretty high penalty charge associated with it. Have a discussion with your banking representative to ask if you might qualify for this protection.

BILL PAYMENT METHODS

All bills (other than your rent cheque) can be paid through the ATM machine, which is cheaper than paying the in-person teller fee. You can do Internet banking or call the telephone banking service 24/7 to pay your bills as well (the number is usually on the back of your debit card). All of Canada's big five banks offer it. You simply give them all of your service provider billing account information to set it up. Very convenient!

The Worst Financial Time of the Month

Your rent payment date is the worst financial time of the month because for most of us it is our largest monthly bill payment. When that payment is due, it can be hard to pay your other financial commitments. If you have a job where you get paid every two weeks, you might want to consider budgeting out all your bills (phone, cable, utilities, loan payments, credit card payments, car payments, etc.) and pay a portion of them every two weeks, the day after payday. This will lessen the major once-a-month financial shock. Check your bills, though — sometimes amounts vary and they can be more than you expected. Companies will list their phone number on the bill, and you can call to find out the balance owing. This can help you to ensure that your bi-monthly payments work out correctly.

Debt, Income, and Student Loans

Many financial planners will tell you that some debt is good: such as debt for your education, for a house, or a car; and that some debt is stupid: for gadgets, clothing, beauty services, plastic surgery, or vacations that you haven't actually saved up for.

If you are one of the few Canadians who has money saved up for university or college, consider yourself a very blessed person with a significant advantage over the rest of us! If you don't have savings, it is scary but smart to look into borrowing money to achieve a degree. Getting a post-secondary degree is not a race, but it is a requirement for most jobs in today's marketplace. It commonly happens that people end up in jobs totally unrelated to the degree they earned, but it often doesn't matter. The success of having completed a degree shows a prospective employer in any field that you are responsible, that you can handle deadlines and stress, that you can multi-task, do research, read, write, and see things through, among many other hugely important skills that can be applied to any important job.

I completed a four-year university degree and attended a work-study program abroad for two additional years. I did not have any post-secondary education fund saved up when I started out. I received government student loans and I ended up about $35,000 in debt by the time it was over. This was the first time I had ever had a debt. No one had told me about how to deal with debt or even what an interest rate was.

When you are a young adult, or a person changing career paths, wages are relatively low at first, and your income will not go very far, especially if you're living in a major Canadian city and paying 100 percent of your expenses. This makes it very hard to pay back a student loan.

When paying back your loan, it is important for you to try and make more than the minimum payment. For a time I thought I was doing great because I was paying the minimum payment required, as stated on the bill; it was all I could afford anyway. If you just pay the minimum payment, you are likely only paying the interest charge (the fee the bank is charging you for having borrowed the money) or possibly even just a portion of the interest charge. In that case, your principal (the actual amount of your debt before interest charges) will never get reduced and paid off.

If you don't have adequate savings, consider completing your post-secondary degree on a part-time basis so that you can work while studying. Not all degrees can be taken part-time (the one I completed, for example, could not). If you can pay for your education with money you've earned, you'll avoid getting yourself into debt. I can say that as hard as it is to pay back a student loan, it is my personal experience and opinion that incurring debt to achieve a university or college degree is highly worth it because it will give you an advantage in the workplace. Most employers want to see that you have a degree. Canada is ranked number one per capita among the thirty-two member countries in the Organisation for Economic Co-operation and Development (OECD), for individuals with college degrees and number two in the G7 for individuals with university degrees.[3] Therefore, you will most likely need a degree to compete with your peers and land a good job.

Credit and Budget Counselling

Sometimes you can get yourself into a pretty serious financial situation. If it's getting bad and beyond any point you can handle on your own, call and make an appointment to meet with someone in a reputable, non-profit credit counselling organization to ask for confidential, practical assistance. They can help you with budgeting and can help you keep the collection agencies at bay by working with your bill collectors to set up realistic repayment plans that you can afford. Sometimes these agencies might even be able to get the companies to forgive some of the debt you owe. There are many agencies in cities across Canada. Find one through the Ontario Association of Credit Counselling Services, Credit Counselling Society of British Columbia, or Credit Counselling Services of Atlantic Canada; or use Google to search for other such agencies across Canada. Search on the Internet for the one nearest you (see Appendix C).

Your Personal Credit Profile

If you want to know your personal credit profile, which is what companies or landlords may consult to see if you are "credit-worthy," you can use three methods to obtain your report from Equifax® Canada.

---

3   *Invest in Canada*, Flagship Report Summary, 2010.

It is good to check your report from time to time to make sure that nobody is engaging in identity theft and getting loans illegally under your name (e.g., a car lease). You can also try and clear your name if a company mis-reports that you were a bad customer who paid bills late.

- Call 1–800–465–7166. You will need to know your Social Insurance Number to complete the request. Hopefully you won't encounter the problem I had. When I used the automated phone service, the machine did not recognize my saying the "S" in my postal code. I tried to repeat my postal code four times and the machine kept interpreting the "S" as an "F." By that point, the most "clean" word I could use to describe that experience was "frustrating"! I e-mailed them to report the problem, so perhaps it will be fixed in the future.

- You can also visit *www.equifax.ca* to download a form for you to fill out to request your free profile. You will need to mail in your completed form with photocopies of two pieces of government-issued identification (e.g., birth certificate, health card, driver's licence or passport).

- You could buy your credit report on *www.equifax.ca* using a credit card.

- An alternate company offering Canadians a credit profile check is TransUnion®. Visit *www.transunion.ca* for more information.

 # Personal Security

Keys

Consider giving an extra set of your house keys to a friend or family member whom you totally trust. This will be important for that moment when you lose your purse or knapsack or lock your keys inside the car by accident. Again, make absolutely certain that the person you choose is someone you trust completely. When you're at home, it is smartest to keep your doors locked to improve your personal security.

Document Shredder

A document shredder with cross-cutter blades is a major must-have. You should shred all your financial documents — anything with your name, address, financial institution or any other service provider (TV, phone, etc.), because identity theft is a serious threat that, at the very least, can ruin your credit rating, which can stand in the way if you wish to get a loan for a mortgage or a car, or a credit card.

Drinking at a Public Venue

Trust the advice you hear on the news: never leave your drink unattended. There are people who are waiting for an opportunity to drug others and take advantage. They do it quickly, skilfully, and easily. Absolutely anyone can be a victim. If you have to go to the washroom, or get asked to dance with someone, finish your drink first or leave it and get a new one later, even if you think you are leaving it with someone you know. A friend might get up and leave for a similar reason. If someone other than the bartender or server gives you a drink, politely decline. Go out with friends and make sure that you're all accounted for before you leave. Although it's not always possible to go along with the rest (like if someone wants to leave early or super-late), a great code of conduct is to agree to leave with the person you came with, even if for a short period during your outing you are separated from the group while you meet and get to know someone new. Look for signs of any unusual behaviour on the part of your friends and have them watch your back as well. The goal is to have fun, leave, and return home safely.

Driving, Boating, Snowmobiling, or Cycling Sober

Make your best effort to not drink even a sip of alcohol or take even a drag or smallest hit of a drug and drive any vehicle (car, boat, skidoo, bicycle). Just make it a firm rule not to do it, ever, for any reason. It is cool to respect yourself and your friends. Have a plan that includes a designated driver or another way of getting home safely (cab, public transit, friend, parent/guardian) and stick to it.

ALCOHOL OR DRUG AMOUNTS AFFECT EACH PERSON DIFFER-ENTLY. It might even affect you differently than usual if you're over-tired, haven't eaten properly, or if you have taken medication. Be strong enough to stop other people from driving after drinking or taking drugs as well. If you feel it is dangerous for you to stop some-one by asking him or her not to drive or to surrender the car keys, do not be afraid to call the police and report the car colour, make, licence plate, where you are now, and where you suspect the per-son might try and drive. Often when people have consumed alcohol or drugs, their judgment is impaired and they cannot tell they've passed a safe limit.

In the short term, your friend may feel that you've betrayed him or her. There's a small chance that your friendship may be over. In making this call, however, you just might save a life, or more than one life, and it just might be your friend whom you save. If your friendship gets broken from this action, it is still the right choice to make. On the flip side, your friend might come to his/her senses the next day or a few days later and actually thank you for caring.

By the way, the latest drug is the addiction to texting. *Texting while driving is proving to be statistically more lethal than drinking and driving.* In many Canadian provinces, it is a ticketable offence to use your hand-held device while driving anyway. Just wait until you've parked to get the mobile out and text.

Fire Safety and Prevention

- *Stove-top fires and smoking are the leading causes of household fires.* They require your extra care and attention to prevent harm to you as well as to prevent damage to your belongings and to the property.

- *Another major cause of residential fires is alcohol consumption or drug use,* because people's level of alertness and reaction time and their ability to make rational decisions is impaired. Be sober while cooking and smoking. Keep an eye on any others (such as roommates or guests) while they are engaging in these activities.

Kitchen Fires

- *While you are cooking, stay in the kitchen* if you are using oils and high heat. If you turn the cooking temperatures down and you exit the kitchen, come back and check on things regularly. Use a timer, or set your alarm clock, so that you don't forget to come back. Leaving the kitchen, getting distracted, and forgetting to check on your cooking is a major danger and one of the causes of cooking fires.

- *Keep the stove-top and the counter near the stove clear of flammable items* such as paper towels or utensils. These might catch fire if they are near an element that is turned on.

- *Keep a proper fitting lid nearby for the pot or pan you are using.* If you see a small fire in a pot on the stove, put the lid on the pot and turn the element off. These actions will help extinguish the flames.

- *Use your fire extinguisher or throw baking soda or flour onto a stove-top fire.* DO NOT THROW WATER ON IT, AS THIS COULD INCREASE THE FLAMES.

- *If you see a fire in the oven, turn the oven off and keep the oven door closed.* The lack of oxygen could help extinguish the flame. As the flame is dying down, you may want to open the oven door slowly and use your fire extinguisher. Be careful—opening the oven door will increase the flow of oxygen and feed the fire.

- *If wearing a long-sleeve shirt, roll your sleeves up when you're cooking.* Loose-fitting long sleeves can catch fire and cause serious burns to your skin.

- *Buy a multi-purpose, dry chemical fire extinguisher for your kitchen* (usually these are quite small and easy to handle). Take it with you each time you move.

Smoking-Related Fires

- Wet cigarette butts thoroughly before depositing them into large metal cans.

- Keep an eye on roommates or partiers who are not sober or who might have fallen asleep. Lit cigarettes that fall onto clothing, furniture such as couches, or carpeting are a leading cause of smoking-related household fires.

Other Household Fires

- *Clothes dryers*: Each home clothes dryer has a dryer filter, which collects a surprising amount of lint from clothing. This lint is something that you really must clean out before you start to dry a new load of laundry because it is one of the leading causes of household fires. The good thing is that it's totally simple to peel off the lint and it only takes about ten seconds. If you don't know where the filter is, ask your landlord or roommate.

- *Candles and incense*: Never leave them burning unattended. Make sure they are fully extinguished when leaving a room.

- *Bathroom appliances*: Unplug curling irons and hair dryers, even if they're turned off.

- *Air conditioning units*: If mounted into a window, ensure that you are using a proper extension cord that is designed specifically for the unit. Using the wrong extension cord, with an inappropriate power gauge, can cause it to overheat and start a fire.

- *Extension cords*: Do not use extension cords as a form of a permanent power supply. Do not staple extension cords into place or put them under carpeting. Both of these actions can cause damage to the cord, which can start a fire.

- *Overloading circuits*: Do not overload circuits by attempting to plug in and use too many appliances at the same time. Use a "power bar" with power surge protection. These have several sockets to plug your items into and the device will turn things off automatically in a power surge.

- *Rodents and pets*: Mice and rats like to chew on electrical cords, and this can cause fires. If you have a rodent problem, eliminate them through pest control. Some pets, such as rabbits and ferrets, also like to chew on electrical cords. Make sure they are caged appropriately.

Smoke Detectors

- The landlord should provide smoke detectors.

- "Ionization" smoke detectors should be placed on every level of a house and one outside each bedroom. Since ionization detectors are sensitive to steam and cooking, these are not ideal for placing near kitchens and bathrooms because you will end up with a lot of false alarms.

- "Photo-sensitive" smoke detectors are the best choice to place near your kitchen or bathroom because they are not sensitive to steam.

- Do occasional checks of the smoke detectors by pressing the test button to make sure they are operating properly.

- Change the batteries every year, using a memorable date like the Daylight Savings Time change or your birthday.

Escaping a Fire and Getting Help

- If a fire is getting big fast, exit the residence, closing doors behind you as you leave in order to limit the spreading of the fire.

- If the apartment is filled with smoke, cover your nose and mouth with clothing or a towel, stay low to the ground where there will be less smoke, and exit by crawling.

- Call 911 from outside the residence and ask for fire services. If you are injured, ask for an ambulance as well.

- If you are renting in an apartment building, pull the fire alarm to warn others. Exit the residence using the stairs.

Fire-Escape Planning

- If you're looking at renting a basement apartment, make sure there are windows you could climb out of in case of emergency (e.g., if a fire blocked your door).

- Think about your fire-escape plan. Each new place you move into will have its own escape options and challenges that you need to think about in advance of an emergency situation.

- Consider visiting the Ottawa Fire Services Web site. It has information about fire safety and prevention in cases of high-rise apartment fires, barbequing on balconies, how to use a fire extinguisher, home fire-escape planning, etc. *www.ottawa.ca/ residents/fire/index_en.html.*

When I was seventeen, I found a listing in the city newspaper for a shared apartment that was just a twenty-minute drive from my house. I was so excited to move out on my own. In a way, my new place was a bit like home in that I had my own room (luckily I could have my own TV in there) and I shared the other rooms with everyone else. I was a bit nervous because I was the new guy in the house and I was younger than the other two guys and the lady who were already renting there. I didn't actually know how to do basic things like cooking. My mom had cooked me a full breakfast every single day (eggs, bacon, French toast) and she had done my laundry. I found out that I didn't need to worry because my roommates were all very nice. Nobody cared what time I came and went. They showed me how to use the washer and dryer and they were also very social, so we often had parties at the house, and on occasion it got a bit rowdy.

One morning in January, I woke up with a bit of a hangover. I didn't want to get out of bed so I pulled the covers over my head. A short while later, I was pretty sure that I could smell smoke. I got up, looked around the kitchen in case someone's toast was burning or something, checked the appliances, and checked the furnace in the basement. I couldn't find anything wrong so I went and watched TV in the living room. Then the smoke smell seemed to be getting stronger and totally overwhelming. I went back to my bedroom and when I opened the door it was full of smoke. I closed the door and called 911; the firemen came, rushed to my room, and emerged with my mattress.

They dragged my mattress, covered by my blanket, outside onto the lawn. It was obvious that a corner of my mattress had caught on fire from a halogen lamp that fell on it (there was no lampshade—just a bulb). The firemen told me to leave the mattress outside to air out. That night it snowed 40 centimetres, burying my mattress completely! I slept on the couch for a week and I also slept at a friend's apartment for a bit. The clothes in my room stank of smoke for a long time. Because we had apartment insurance, I got a new mattress, and the walls were repainted. We shovelled the mattress out in April, which is when the mystery of the disappearance of the remote control for my TV was solved: it had been stuck between the mattress and the blanket for four months!

When I look back at that story now, I wish we had had more smoke alarms in our place. I also feel very grateful that the whole event didn't happen at night while I was sleeping!

Yves
Moncton, New Brunswick

Travelling

DOCUMENT YOUR TRAVELS. It's a good idea to let someone you know of the dates of your travel and where you're going. As well, give someone you trust a copy of your passport, birth certificate, and any special travel medical insurance documentation (a must-purchase!) in case of accident or injury or loss of personal documentation while you're travelling. These backups can help you get emergency replacements or emergency care. Canadians do not have health care coverage abroad. An unanticipated visit to a foreign hospital could cost you thousands of dollars if you have not obtained insurance. Medical insurance can be purchased through Blue Cross® or many of Canada's major banks, and it's very inexpensive.

WRITING THE EMERGENCY CONTACT INFORMATION IN YOUR PASSPORT IN LEGIBLE PENCIL is a good idea. Canadian passports are valid for five years. The person you choose to note as your emergency contact in year one might change in year four or five. Also, his/her address and phone number might change.

COVER YOUR TRACKS: ASK SOMEONE TO PICK UP YOUR MAIL so that it doesn't accumulate outside in your mailbox and attract the wrong kind of attention from potential thieves. In terms of your lighting, you could purchase automatic timer gadgets to turn your lights on and off at different intervals to hide the fact that you're travelling.

IF YOU WILL BE TRAVELLING TO A FOREIGN COUNTRY, REGISTER YOURSELF ON THE REGISTRATION OF CANADIANS ABROAD (ROCA) WEB SITE (Google it). When you register here, it helps the Government of Canada's emergency response team to locate you and offer you help to get home in a time of crisis (such as the sudden eruption of civil war in Lebanon, in which the Canadian government brought our citizens home, the recent Haiti earthquake, or a family emergency).

IF YOU'RE IN TROUBLE ABROAD — WHO YOU GONNA CALL? (No, it's not Ghostbusters!) If you find yourself in any kind of trouble with foreign authorities (like the police) while you're abroad, you can get help from the Canadian government through Canadian consulates or embassies in the country you're visiting. E-mail *sos@international. gc.ca* or call collect: such a call from most countries will be accepted by a Government of Canada representative at 613–996–8885. (You speak to the telephone operator and say, "I'd like to make a collect call to Canada. The number is 613–996–8885," so you won't have to pay the long-distance charge. The Government of Canada will agree to pay for the call and will assist you.) This service is just one of the many reasons to love your country and your government!

Grocery Shopping

As a person living on your own, you'll most likely find that without proper grocery planning and buying, food can go bad if you buy too much. It takes a lot of practice buying just the right amount. Try to aim for a variety from one week to the next, rather than a whole lot of variety each week. If possible, try to live somewhere within walking distance to the grocery store or greengrocer. This way you can buy a little bit now and then again when you need it.

Unless you live on Canada's West Coast where the climate is warmer and the fruits and vegetables can be grown for longer periods throughout the year, you will find that most of the nutrition in the fruit and vegetable aisle comes from the United States, China, Australia, Brazil, Mexico, etc. It never used to be like this in Canada. The food we now buy is usually harvested before it was ripe (likely reducing the nutrients and certainly reducing the flavour), was shipped very, very long distances by vehicles using oil that pollutes the environment during transport, and may have been packaged using chemical preservatives. Some fruits and vegetables may be sprayed to ripen upon time of delivery. However, I am not an agri-food expert so I cannot discuss this with any certainty. You could consider researching this if you are interested.

It is true that every single person can have an impact. Whenever possible, buy food grown as locally as possible, from your own province or territory, or at least from somewhere in Canada. The best option is to shop at the local farmers' markets. Always choose locally grown food that is in season, even if it costs dozens of cents more at the checkout counter. The reason is that it will be more nutritious, more flavourful, it will have been grown and harvested by the few skilled agriculture experts we still have, on fertile agricultural land that has not been ploughed over with homes and stores. At a farmers' market you can also ask the farmer questions about how the food was grown, how to cook it, and how to store it so that it will last longer. It's a nice opportunity to thank them as well. Farming is very hard work. Try volunteering on a farm — you will probably be surprised how physically intensive the work is. Farmers deserve our thanks and our support by (at least) buying their products.

If you have some gardening space, consider growing some of your own food with "heirloom seeds." Heirloom seeds are those held in the public domain (owned by the people), traded and sold between farmers and gardeners. They are an alternative to those seeds owned and genetically modified by corporations, which typically require pesticide applications (chemicals also owned by corporations).

I quote Dan Jason when he asks, "O Canada, How Can We Grow for Thee?" This guy's "The Zero Mile Diet Seed Kit" for forty-six dollars sounds really cool. It's got thirteen seed packets, a twenty-page growing guide, and a recipe book. He offers non-genetically modified seeds that are organically grown. Visit *www.saltspringseeds.com* for more information. Make sure the seeds can be grown in your ecological zone.

If you are a person who enjoys eating meat, try to buy your meat from local farmers or from a real butcher shop because then you can avoid buying meat stored on Styrofoam. Not only are Styrofoam trays not all capable of being recycled, other garbage pressures include the cellophane wrap and diaper-type padding under the meat. Seems gross to me!

Food Banks

There may be times when financially you just can't make ends meet. Everyone has to eat — that includes you! So, you pay the essentials first, like your rent. If you can't afford groceries, go to a food bank. You can find food banks in the phone book or on the Internet. Go to your closest food bank. When you arrive to ask for some groceries, you will need to present some personal identification and proof of your address. For some people it will feel very sad and shameful to admit that they need help to feed themselves, but don't you worry about this. There may be times in your life that you need help and there will also be times when you're doing okay and you can donate food for others. Canada is a society that believes strongly in assisting each other. There is every reason that you should receive help when you need it.

Making Your Own Fast Food

Try doing a major cook once or twice a week. You could fry up a large portion of basic "aromatics" such as onions, garlic, celery, herbs, mushrooms, and salt and pepper. Sometimes adding a splash of lemon can really brighten it up; or in other dishes, adding drops of toasted sesame oil can help you have a totally different meal from the same basics. Once cooked, set these aromatics aside. Ideally, these basics that you've cooked should be enough to add to three different types of meals. To avoid boredom, you could switch celery with fennel, or change the mushrooms with carrots, or add green peppers, or throw a few bean sprouts on top at the last minute, maybe with a different sauce like (lower sodium) Tamari.

You can divvy up these aromatics into spaghetti sauce as one option, lentil stew as another option, and, say, chicken with couscous as a third. Basically, try to make enough to have several portions of each different dish. Separate out the meals into different single-portion containers and, once they have cooled down a bit, put them in the freezer. This way you reduce your overall cooking time throughout the week and can avoid "meal repeat boredom." You can have a super-busy few days and just warm something up in the microwave in three minutes, whether at university, work, or at home at night. Be sure not to heat the food in the plastic containers; small amounts of chemicals in the plastic can leach into your food.

Plastic food containers can be purchased affordably but try to save up so that now and then you can replace them with glass containers. Glass containers will last for as long as you can avoid breaking them. Glass is great because it doesn't stain like plastic (worst offender is tomato sauce) and then when you re-heat the contents you won't have to transfer the food to a glass container first. The important thing to know is to not put the plastic lid on when you are reheating the food in the microwave. Just don't fill the food right up to the top — then it won't bubble up and spill over and cause a mess in the microwave. If your lid breaks, then you can re-purpose the glass container into a bowl or serving dish.

If you don't have one by now, buy yourself a reusable lunch bag. I like mine. It has a lower zipper pouch for the main course and a separate one (for the salad, fruit or dessert or for a second main course if you know you're going to be out for lunch *and* dinner). It is super handy, and I generally save a lot of money by planning well and cooking ahead so I don't have to eat out.

The average young person is not a good cook (myself included)! Consider watching a friend or family member making something or take a course. When you live alone and cook for yourself all the time, it can be easy to get into a cooking rut. Try looking up a new recipe on the Internet or asking a friend for their best no-fail recipe to incorporate a bit of change into your typical menu. If you like something at a restaurant, the chef might even tell you the ingredients and how to cook it if you muster up enough courage and ask politely.

When I was eighteen, I moved from my Six Nations reserve to London so that I could go to college. I looked up apartments for rent in the newspaper, grabbed a map, and my cousin and I left the reserve to look for a place to live in the big city. I found a bachelor apartment for $425, which was affordable. It was a tiny place, but it was mine. Later I realized that I was living in a totally sketchy neighbourhood. In retrospect, I think it would have been a good idea to talk to one of the locals (such as staff at the college) beforehand about where the best parts of the city were and which neighbourhoods to avoid.

I didn't have much to furnish my place so I went to a big box store to buy the necessities. I remember thinking—this is better than Christmas! I had a ton of new stuff. My family helped me pack and move to my new apartment.

I was completely overwhelmed by moving out. I had left the rez, where I knew everyone and had a hundred cousins, to move to a place where I knew absolutely no one. I had had my first and only non-Native friend in Grade 9 and going to college made me learn how to be open to meeting a whole lot of people who were not part of my culture. I experienced sleeping in my own place by myself for the first time. I also had to learn how to take a city bus and figure out how to stretch my dollar to fit my budget. One of the tricks I learned was to borrow movies and CDs from the local library. They actually get in all the new releases and you can borrow them for free! My dad always taught us to buy car, home (apartment), and life insurance, so I made sure to factor that into my budget.

As well, I had to learn how to grocery shop and cook for myself. In those early days, I became a big Kraft Dinner eater because it was cheap and easy to make but I soon started to feel really lethargic and suspected it might be my poor nutrition fast-food choices. I got myself a cookbook and managed to learn how to make some basic things and get more vegetables into my diet. I discovered that this was better brain food and it actually even helped me sleep better, too. Overall, moving out on your own for the very first time is a bit like sink or swim—you've just got to figure it out!

Cynthia, Six Nations, Ontario

 # End-of-Life Issues

A Living Will

Not to be morbid or anything, but it does happen that people die unexpectedly. Of course, we pray this won't be you or anyone in your family, but the reality is that sooner or later we will all die. You may want to buy a living will kit, for example from Chapters/ Indigo bookstores or Staples. I bought mine there for twenty dollars. It is cheaper than hiring a lawyer, and these forms are totally legal in Canada (with the exception of Quebec, where the legal system is different). They are a way of ensuring that your end-of-life requests will be respected. What if you want to give some of your possessions to someone? How do you want to be buried? Do you want to be cremated? It is a document that can speak for you when you can't speak for yourself.

Funeral Costs—WATCH OUT!

Besides an emotional shock, funeral services can represent a huge financial shock. You might feel like someone is committing highway robbery against you and you really wouldn't be far off the mark. Perhaps you come from a small family and you'll need to get involved in helping to plan and pay for the burial of a loved one. Recently I asked for a quote on picking up the deceased person, issuing the death certificate, providing a two-hour memorial service, and purchasing a moderately priced casket. The price quoted was $8,400 before taxes (a Toronto price). This didn't even include charges for opening the ground and paying for the real estate (land for the body's burial). Plan in advance for family members and for yourself; consider getting a membership to your local funeral information / advisory society as a good place to start.

Funeral Information / Advisory Societies

Why the heck am I harping on about death and funeral services? What a downer! Believe me when I say that I am not some anxiety-ridden freak walking around thinking about this! I first learned about my local society when I attended a green/eco fair in my neighbourhood. I was kind of shocked to see a booth with a funeral information society representative. What the heck was he doing there, I wondered? He was presenting information about green/eco burial options, which I had never heard about before. I didn't know that you can be buried in a shroud (like a blanket) instead of a casket, or that there is a process called "reformation," whereby most of your body can be reduced to a liquid. I also didn't know how toxic embalming a body is, and that maybe those chemicals shouldn't be put into the earth. I didn't know that there are only two official green/eco cemeteries in Canada where people buried there agree not to be embalmed and not to be placed in a casket made from unsustainable wood products.

I didn't know that if the body is cremated, you can place the ashes free of charge on Crown (government) land, such as a national park. There were lots of things I didn't know and still don't know—I'm learning.

The funeral industry is a hugely lucrative, rather secretive business sector. You can't exactly Google different funeral service prices. There are networks in many major Canadian cities called Funeral Information / Funeral Advisory Societies that you can join and become a member of (in each city there are slightly different names for the local network).

Part of the benefit of being a member of a funeral information society (costing usually a one-time fee of around forty-five dollars) is that you can have someone to talk through your questions with. Death and funeral planning is not exactly the kind of topic you can bring up at the dinner table. Talking about death is largely taboo and just way too sad. A society representative can tell you the full range of funeral costs from the least expensive to the most expensive options. By becoming a member in my city I became privy to a price list of services. I saw price ranges from $600 to $3,500 for the same services. Nobody wants to be "cheap," but you don't have to get "taken to the cleaners" when you're totally distraught, either. Should you wish to learn about end-of-life issues, maybe you'd like to consider joining your local society. (See Appendix D for society contact information across Canada.)

Organ Donation

Consider signing up to be an organ donor. In the unfortunate event that you die, you may be able to give the gift of life to others or support medical research. One organ donor can possibly save the lives of eight Canadians and improve the lives of up to fifty more, depending on the quality of health of the donor's organs and tissues. If you decide you'd like to be a donor, inform your family that this is important to you. If they don't know about your wishes, they may override your decision in this matter at the time of death. To obtain more information on organ donation and any special ways of registering in your province or territory, visit the Canadian Association of Transplantation at *www.transplant.ca* where you can download a donor card.

PART II

The Emotional and Social Aspects of Living on Your Own

Success

The point is to figure out how to live alone as successfully as you can in order to be a happy person. Success can mean different things to different people but there's generally something about success that holds true for everyone: success feels good.

You will likely go through some periods of intense energy and achievement in an area that you have a natural strength in. In these periods you probably will actually accomplish some things either for yourself or for society that are easily recognizable as success. There is no one else in the world who can tell you what success will mean to you with certainty, but you can learn to recognize what this is for yourself by trusting your feelings and by reviewing the results of your actions. It will be easier to live on your own at these times because you'll likely have high personal confidence and feel satisfied and proud of yourself to some degree. This is the ideal scenario.

Dealing with the Blue Times

A lot of people go through life with an optimistic, easy, carefree attitude, which is great. It is totally natural that besides the periods of success and general happiness, there will be "down" times as well, when you may not feel happy or feel that you are not achieving anything significant in your life.

LIVING LIFE IS NOT ALWAYS ABOUT THE BIG STUFF unless you are a major change agent in the world (such as, for example, a volunteer or a worker in a social development or ecological restoration organization). Many days in our lives are about experiencing the little, simple things, and it is best if you can feel like you are able to take care of yourself (e.g., cooking your meals, washing your dishes, doing your exercise), that you are connected to people you know and love (keeping relationships with family and friends), and that you can present yourself with pride to the world (good personal hygiene; good personal grooming; nice, clean clothing, ironed if necessary). These little things should not be underestimated because although on the surface they may seem insignificant, when they're added up they actually do enable you to be a successful person in your own eyes and in the eyes of society.

IT MIGHT NOT BE VERY CANADIAN TO GO AROUND FISHING FOR COMPLIMENTS, BUT THE MOMENTS IN TIME THAT YOU WILL RECEIVE FEEDBACK ABOUT DOING ANYTHING GOOD MAY NEVER COME OR THEY MAY BE RARE AND DELIVERED TO YOU SPORADI-CALLY. If you have a lousy job, or if you're surrounded by friends going through rough patches, you might actually be the recipient of negative comments (most likely for reasons that are totally unjust). If this happens, just try to remove yourself from those negative situations, take a deep breath and realize that the negativity may not even be about you. Take a moment to believe in yourself and move on if you can. Aim for better. Do you remember how you felt when a teacher commended you for doing good work? Or when your parent, or coach, or co-worker, or friend gave you a compliment? Although it may sound stupid and trivial on the surface, it is actually pretty important for us to receive validation for being a good person and for doing things well.

SOMETIMES IT IS HELPFUL TO TRY WRITING DOWN A SHORT LIST OF YOUR OWN GOOD ACCOMPLISHMENTS in a given day. This is not an exercise to adhere to as a lifelong mission! Just for the blue, lonely times when life just doesn't really seem to be about too much, and when you are not getting that occasional pat on the back from others. It may sound kind of lame and stupid but it's a simple, private tool that can actually make a difference to your mental well-being by helping you take the time to realize that you're actually doing okay.

Doing something good in a day can be as little as:

❏ I flossed my teeth

❏ I spoke with someone in my family

❏ I phoned a friend I hadn't talked to in a long time

❏ I apologized because I did something wrong

❏ I put the recycling out

❏ I paid my bills

❏ I ironed my clothes

❏ I remembered to take my cloth bags when I went shopping

❏ I stopped and looked at art in a store/gallery

❏ I turned off the TV and listened to music

❏ I cooked some meals for the week

❏ I cleaned the fridge

❏ I spent time reading a book or a newspaper

❏ I volunteered my time somewhere to help others

When written down and reflected upon, accomplishments like these can help give you a small boost to feel good about yourself. When you live alone, no one is going to help you acknowledge that you are actually doing okay — you have to be capable of affirming this to yourself. This list can be something you shred or burn later so that no one finds it. If this sounds too silly for you to write stuff down, try picking up the phone and talking about your feelings to a good friend who lives alone. He/she will probably totally understand what you're talking about and will feel grateful that you're sharing what you're going through.

# Friendships

FRIENDSHIPS ARE VITALLY IMPORTANT WHEN YOU ARE A PERSON WHO LIVES ON YOUR OWN because, if you are not living with a boyfriend or girlfriend or roommates who are your friends, you're essentially living through much of your personal life alone. You'll need to interact with others to help you understand and process things, to share your positive and challenging experiences, and to get good advice. While in high school or college or university, you will have an easily accessible network of friends. When you're not in school it can be harder to develop a solid circle of friends. As well, as your friends start to get married and have kids it can be harder to remain friends because people get busy.

When I was eighteen, my parents helped me move into residence when I went to university. Moving was hell because I was so sick with strep throat that day. I shared a modest room with another girl on an all-girls floor. My dorm-mate was really nice and we got really silly together. We'd often sing Disney songs and gossip about people we knew before we fell asleep. It was nice living in residence because there were always lots of people around and you never felt lonely. I really hated that the shared kitchen was in the basement. It was a bummer to have to carry your plates and cutlery down there when you wanted to eat. One time I actually ate cold soup from a can because I just didn't feel like going down there. On the bright side, though — the basement level was an all-male floor so I got to check out all the cute guys.

Natalie
Hamilton, Ontario

There is a lot to be said on the subject of friendships. The guidance below is really just a snapshot of thoughts a person living on her/his own can consider when selecting or interacting with friends. I will also outline my perspective on a few of the trickier "friend situations" for you to consider, in case you find yourself going through them and would like an outsider's perspective.

Developing Your Friend Network

Friendships develop to varying degrees, with close friends, not-so-close friends, new acquaintances, family members, pseudo-family members, pets, work colleagues, and others you just meet out of the blue.

In order to have optimal friend support, it is best to aim to have friends with a variety of good qualities, such as those who are well-educated, balanced, optimistic, engaging, active, curious, analytical, successful, handy, funny, health-conscious, sporty, creative, and talented, etc., because they will enrich you in your life and will likely give you advice and support that you can trust will be good for you. Of course, no one person can be strong in all of those qualities, which is why it's good for you to find them in a variety of friends.

Friends are most often found through school, work, church or synagogue, clubs, hobbies, or neighbours. They can also be found at community or cultural centres. For example, many of Canada's indigenous peoples (First Nation, Métis and Inuit) may find a good support network through "Friendship Centres." Others might feel connected to places like the Jewish Community Centres or public municipal recreation centres. There are also excellent on-line social networks like Facebook and *www.meetup.com* (with groups in your city organized by age or hobby interest) that can serve as a platform to connect with others. These are especially helpful if you're moving to a new city and are far away from established friends.

I grew up in a family with three other sisters. My mom had a very direct way of sharing her philosophy about how to grow up. Our high school graduation gift from Mom was a set of suitcases! With just a high school diploma, it's common to get out of Whitehorse if you want a better job than pumping gas. So there I was, at age seventeen, a Yukonner trying to figure out how to go out and make it in the world. At that age I had no idea what I wanted to study at university. I was really lucky to be awarded an opportunity to participate in the Rotary Club Student Exchange and so I went and lived in Argentina for a year. It was great because it gave me something to focus on. I met other exchangers and Argentineans who were very different than the people I grew up with, some of whom continue to be my friends. After that program was over, I kind of had an idea of what I wanted to study, so I came back to Canada and went to university in Nova Scotia.

Nicole
Whitehorse, Yukon

The "Blue Moon" Call

The blue moon call happens "once in a blue moon" and is a call you make to a person you haven't talked to in ages — sometimes years. You flip through your phone book or your photo album and you just decide: Today I'm going to call this person, say hello, and see how it goes. These are usually very interesting calls, and the person on the other end is typically very happy that you made the effort. These calls usually don't result in a close buddy-buddy relationship all of a sudden. They are usually something like a little glimpse into someone's life — a short update. It's a brief moment of joy — if you're lucky. It's a kind of take-a-chance situation — a little point of reconnection and an opportunity for reflection.

You May Be Cool but Sometimes They Just Ain't Goin' to Like You . . .

Oh no, did I say that out loud? Even though you may think that you are a good and cool person, which you likely are in your own special way, the reality is that not everyone is going to like you no matter what you do. Everybody has his/her own personal reasons for this. It can be chemical, a vibe, looks, perception of being too fat or too thin, too tall or too short, economic status, religious difference, race, stereotypes, education level, fear, perception of being too competitive or too shy, difference of general interests, difference of political opinion, different tastes in comedy or artistic interests, or fear of your physical or mental illness. It can be about the friends you hang out with, the clothes you choose, sexual orientation, physical ability, disability or disfigurement, where you work, and so on. In short, it can be for any combination of superficial and non-superficial reasons. This is natural. Just accept it. On the flip side, many of these unique attributes are actually reasons that people WILL like you! The number of people in the world is in the billions. There absolutely will be people in this world whom you can connect with in a beautiful way. Just make an effort to find them and let go of those who have no meaningful and positive connection for you.

What to Share with Friends

Remember that friendship is not all about sharing the burdensome things. Don't forget to connect with your friends about the joyful, positive things as well — otherwise they might feel like you're just dumping the bad stuff on them all the time, and that can be a big and tiring responsibility for a listener and supporter. You could burn out your friends to the point that they decide they can't deal with you or simply don't want to be your friend any more. What's up with you? What are your dreams and goals?

 # Friend Troubles and Friend Drama Scenarios

Having Friends Is Not Always a Straight and Easy Road

Sometimes it can be confusing when things don't go all rosy. Sometimes things go wrong with friends either for a good reason or sometimes just because of a misunderstanding of intentions. There is often no way to know in advance — you will just know when it happens. If it happens and you get a chance to apologize, you might be able to fix it together through openness, honesty, and communication. Other times you may not get a chance to apologize. Just think about it as a lesson learned and try not to repeat that behaviour again. Or try not to put yourself in a situation with another person like that again. Learn to let go and move on without revenge or self-loathing. Everyone has lessons to learn. Sometimes it's the one you're going through.

I moved out on my own when I was twenty-three. I rented a basement apartment by myself in a house. It had its own private entrance. I noticed a kind of a weird smell in the place but I didn't think too much of it. One day, one of my co-workers said something to me about how my clothes smelled like mould or mildew or something. I didn't really know what that was, exactly. I told my landlord and he came downstairs and lifted some of the carpeting. He saw the tell-tale signs, replaced one of the carpets, and gave me a dehumidifier. There was so much dampness down there that it pulled a lot of water out of the air and I had to empty it a lot.

At that time I was dating a guy, and our relationship progressed to the point that we wanted to live together. My landlord didn't want anyone else to move in with me so my boyfriend and I had to look for another place. We found a pretty classy and expensive apartment. We signed a one-year lease and pooled our money to pay the first and last month's rent. Moving day came, and my mom and dad helped me move. In one trip I moved half my stuff into the new apartment. Then I got a call from my boyfriend. He told me at that moment that he decided he wasn't ready to move in with me and that he wasn't going to. I tried to reason with him but he was firm in his decision. I started crying and I went to see the property manager and explained the situation to him. Maybe it was because my parents were there with me and because I was honest about the whole fiasco, that he agreed to allow me to break my lease and he returned the last month's rent portion. My parents and I repacked my stuff and I moved right back into the basement. That boyfriend was a total jerk. He and I didn't last much longer after that.

Niki
Ottawa, Ontario

I've moved a few times. One time I decided to move in with my boyfriend. Then he lost his job. He was trying to find work and he was really stressed out. Since I had a nine-to-five job, I paid the rent for both of us. Our agreement was that at the very least he would help clean up around the house; but cleaning was not his "style." One day I came home and I found Kraft Dinner powder all over the bathroom sink. I asked him: "So how come there's all this KD powder in here?" He told me it was because there were too many dirty dishes in the kitchen sink! In the end he got a job, I helped him find his own place, and then I broke up with him.

Lynn
Ottawa, Ontario

I Thought We Were Going to Be "Best Friends" Forever

Friends you are certain are your "best friends" may stay with you for life. The reality for most people is that many will not. Many friends come into a person's life for a short period of time (or perhaps for what some might call a "cosmic reason"). The best of friends will be those you call and can just pick up a conversation with, without feeling that you've ever really been apart too long. The important thing is to try and find and keep two or three friends you can be totally open and honest with about anything. You will want to be able to talk through your joys, challenges, and most secret things with someone who can listen and offer you some support, perspective, good advice, or comfort.

The Drifting-Apart Friend Scenario

You might find that you and some of your friends drift apart. This is natural, especially if you have a friend who starts dating someone; or who gets married and starts a family; or who gets a new pet. They just get totally consumed with their new love life and family life and tend to forget you either in part or altogether. Other reasons can include illness, depression, work stress, changing jobs, financial stress, a move, or a death in their family or of a close friend. Losing a friend is sometimes not all about you, or what you've said or done. Sometimes it is about what your friend is going through. Sometimes, however, it is perfectly acceptable to feel that you are changing and that it is you who needs to be a part of a different circle of friends.

It is natural that some friends or family members might stop reaching out to you, and it is normal for you to feel disappointed or sometimes even hurt or angry. If your friend or family member stops calling, just suspect that there could be a reason other than that they don't care about you and cut them some slack. If there's enough of a reason to stay friends or to stay connected, just try to occasionally get in touch and arrange a get-together or a chat by phone. When this happens, let things cool off for a while and look to others for friendship. You likely have a bigger network than you realize. Sometimes it is just a matter of activating it by finding a little courage to take the first step and reach out.

You're Always the Caller

Some people are just not naturally prone to reaching out although you can tell that they enjoy your company and are happy when you call them. You might feel it is worth it for you to be the one who always calls them. You could let them know that you do hope they will call you now and then (as a prompt); they might get the hint that you would like them to make an effort. If they do, remember to thank them for calling, as it is likely that they have actually made a special effort to do so.

With some other friends, you may decide that you're tired of always being the caller; in that case, it is perfectly natural to decide to let that friendship die. If this happens, try not to be a hater. Life is long. People change. You will change. Circumstances change. Who knows? There may be an opportunity for your friendship to come alive once again in the future.

Obviously, I haven't brought up all aspects of friendships because I can't, and because this is not a book about friendship! As an alternative to sharing with friends, it might also be an option for you to reach out to a spiritual or religious advisor or mentor for support.

Dealing with the Death of a Friend or Family Member

It is an unfortunate and terrible and natural reality that people we know are going to die, either suddenly and unexpectedly or slowly and painfully due to diseases like cancer.

It can be very hard and perhaps more lengthy to get through the emotional pain when you grieve as a person who lives on your own because you won't have someone to come home to, to help comfort you or to distract you into focusing on something else. Hang in there and reach out to friends or family or spiritual/religious counsellors for support.

Natural Emotional Reactions to Death

We all react to the passing of a close personal friend, family member, or even somewhat close friends or family members in our own ways. Perhaps you may experience something like any of the following feelings:

- Shock that the person you know died — especially if they passed away far too young
- Extreme sadness and pain at the loss
- Strong emotional waves of disbelief
- Surprise that it doesn't affect you too much and you wonder if you are a cold and hard person without a heart
- Thoughts that you want to commit suicide (If you are considering this action, know that you are special and that you are not alone. There is hope for you. Please reach out for support. See Appendix E for suicide-prevention personal support hotline phone numbers.)
- Satisfaction if you feel certain that they lived a good and long life and you understand that it was their time
- Closer and more connected to the person who passed away than you ever did before

Sometimes a death will change you and inspire you to change or grow or to continue a hobby or volunteer work that your loved one / friend enjoyed.

A death may prompt you to consider how to behave toward others in general. The ideal scenario is when you feel that you behaved nicely and respectfully toward that person when you had the chance. Were you nice to him (or her) when you spoke together? Did you ever help him in some little way? Did you honour him by following his advice or activate something he taught you? Did you help him feel confident that he was good at something or did you give him a compliment and tell him that he looked really good or did a great job? Did you sing him a song or give him a hug?

If you keep this in mind, it might help you to remember to always try your best to behave well toward others. It may also encourage you to tell people close to you that you love them, even if it's only when you sign a card "Love" . . . You just never know, it may actually be significant for you one day and it may help you as you live through your grieving process.

I rented a basement apartment from an East Indian couple. They were very nice. When I got sick, they brought food downstairs to me. It was so sad when the lady passed away from cancer, because I had gotten to know her and like her. When she passed, a lot of their friends and family came over and brought food—just like how it is in my Shuswop First Nations culture. The husband couldn't eat all the food people brought so he gave some to me.

In general, there's not a lot of air circulation in basement apartments because you're pretty much underground, and there can be quite a cold and damp feeling. I got myself a mobile heater, which helped boost the temperature in whatever area I was hanging out in. A major issue in this place was that there ended up being a mould problem because of the dampness, which actually caused the linoleum flooring to pop up. The landlord had to take the flooring out, and I didn't want to stick around to live through that renovation so I gave my notice to move out of the apartment. I remember how hard it was to leave, because the landlord had done some renovations that eliminated the garage door, so I had to lift my bed and couch, etc., out of a regular door, which made it a lot harder than it had been when I moved in.

Cherlyn
Vancouver, B.C.

The Invitation to Hang Out in Your Home

Women and guys are different in so many ways — often in many great ways! It might make sense for a woman to not invite any non-family straight guy into her home, whether he is just a friend, a single person, a person who is in a relationship with a significant other, or a married man. (This rule of thumb could probably be overlooked with gay men.) The reason is this: even when women have no intentions other than to have a friendly chat with a guy, inviting a man into your private space has a high probability of sending an unintended signal that many men will interpret or distort as an invitation to do something more than hang out (given that your space is private and your bedroom is but a few convenient steps away). Of course, we can't paint all men with the same brush. You may be very confident and trustful of a particular person. This is simply a piece of advice for you to spend a moment to think about.

To avoid any misinterpretation, you may consider that the clearest thing is not to invite any man into your home if it is not a group invitation. Hang out with male friends in a public place, unless it's a prospective boyfriend you're pretty confident about taking to the next level! Men can be considerate and respectful on this issue by understanding that a woman is not "dissing" him by not inviting him in. They might even consider it cool that a woman expects to keep their relationship a healthy one.

In general, your home is your own personal space reflecting who you are and how you want to live. The best rule of thumb is to invite only people you really like into it, male or female, to share that part of who you are with them.

Part III

Income Tax,
Eco-friendly Choices,
and Principles
for Living on Your Own
in a Big Canadian City

The Dreaded Income Taxes

Something most people never talk about or mention to a young person starting out is the issue of tax payments. What are personal income taxes and why do people pay taxes? Do you know? I didn't have a clue when I left home. If you grew up in a family like mine or went through an education system like mine, you will likely have very little idea about what taxes are and what the implications are going to be for you.

I have to say outright that I don't have any expertise about taxes. I only have the experience of figuring out what taxes are on my own — and sometimes this was totally about learning it through the school of hard knocks!

Who Pays Income Taxes?

If you earn income from a company, a non-profit organization, or the government, or if you're self-employed — you pay income taxes.

What Do Taxes Pay for, Anyway?

Income taxes are payments we all collectively make to help the Canadian government cover the cost of many things that keep our beautiful Canada a strong and vibrant society. Taxes can pay for some or all of the costs for:

- National museums and art galleries

- Universities (to help keep student tuition lower)

- Scientific research

- Public high schools and elementary schools

- Police forces, courts, judges, and jails

- Major infrastructure investments like sewage and water treatment pipes under city streets

- Major transit systems like subways and national railway systems

- Hospitals
- Doctors' and nurses' salaries
- Senior citizens' residences
- National radio and television broadcasting (such as the CBC and SRC)
- The salaries of the prime minister, governor general, members of Parliament, and government employees
- Arts festivals
- National research, national parks, and environmental protection agencies
- Military defence, border protection, and the Canadian Space Agency
- Financial aid to poor foreign countries or those experiencing a major ecological disaster
- Welfare payments
- Payments to reduce our country's own national debt

Even though it will most likely feel painful to part with the money you've earned, you can probably agree that your tax money helps to cover some very important expenses that enable Canadians to live in a great country. Take some time to consider how beautiful, how cool, and how safe our country is compared to some politically unstable, corrupt, unsafe, violent, dirty, energy-poor, undereducated, and poverty-stricken countries. Canada is one of the best places to live in the world, in part because of what we decide to support through taxation.

Our government leaders are entrusted with ensuring that tax money pays for what our society considers to be of significant importance to running our country and making us a just society with freedom of religion, political thought, and expression; a society that is innovative, creative, educated, vibrant, socially responsible, economically diverse, and viable; and a country that is clean, green, and healthy. This is one of the reasons why it is really important to vote. Every Canadian eighteen years of age and older has a say about how she/he believes our tax money should be spent and who should be responsible to set a future vision for us as a people.

Different political parties have different ideologies, which can ultimately impact how much tax they require workers to pay and what they will use the tax income for. Some parties have stronger social policies (like funnelling investments more into hospitals, general health care, the arts, education) and some have stronger environmental policies. Some want to focus more on reducing the national debt and bolstering national defence. As such, please consider it a high priority for you to have your say and to vote for those individuals and political parties who plan to allocate your tax dollars to the issues you believe will help make our society better.

Basic Income Tax Rules

1. Do not think you can evade taxes. No one can — not even people who die during the taxation year.

2. File your income tax return by April 30 (if you're self-employed you can do your return by June 15 but any money owed has to be paid by April 30 to avoid penalty charges). For example, on April 30, 2011, you report all the income you earned from January 1, 2010, to December 31, 2010.

3. Plan for it — you are going to owe taxes every single year unless you are really poor, in which case you will qualify for a refund payment from society's social safety net (derived from tax payments made by others).

4. If at some point in the year you move from one province/ territory to a different one, you will be taxed at the rate of the province/territory you lived in on December 31 of the taxation year.

5. In some provinces/territories, you only have to do the federal income tax return; the provincial/territorial tax portion gets transferred automatically. In some places, like Quebec, you have to file a federal tax return and complete and file your provincial tax return separately. Be sure you do all the necessary tax returns.

6. Tax laws change from year to year — if not every year, then every couple or every few years. This is one of its tricky points.[4]

How to Get Your Income Tax Return Done

1. You can go to a reputable tax return company that has a storefront in your neighbourhood (such as H & R Block®).

2. You can hire a certified personal or corporate income tax accountant; go with someone you've been referred to. If you run your own business, the money you pay the accountant to do your tax return can be written off in the next tax year as a legitimate business expense.

3. You can use an on-line software program.

4. You can use the free paper filing booklet that you'll find in the Canada Post office.

The safest thing to do is to hire a professional, because you'll know where you stand and you'll get it done right. Hiring a company like H & R Block® or a certified professional accountant can also make sure that you are claiming all the deductions possible to give you the best advantage.

---

4   For current changes, refer to the Canada Revenue Agency Web site, www.cra-arc. gc.ca.

How Long Do You Have to Keep Your Tax Records?

We all need to keep our annual tax records for seven years (the year that you filed the tax return plus the six previous years). So, you are going to need a system to keep these records and lug them around with you every time you move. Annual envelopes that contain the return and all related receipts and tax slips, stored in one large plastic box, may be an easy option.

Getting Audited

Guess what? You will likely experience one or more tax audits by the government within a seven-year period. "Getting audited" means that the government can write to you and demand that you show them all your tax and income slips and records of any other amounts you've claimed as special deductions. They do this because they want to make sure that you've done your income tax return correctly, but more likely it is because they suspect that you may not have paid all the taxes owed.

Beware, the Canada Revenue Agency (1–800–959–8281) can write to you two, three, four, five, six, or even seven years later and ask that you show your records to them. So, remember to keep your records; it is a real potentiality. When your records are older than the seven-year mark, you can shred them or you could just hang onto them. Throwing them into the recycling bin is not an option, due to the high risk of identity fraud if the wrong person gets hold of this information!

What if You're Self-Employed?

If you decide to start your own business, no one will deduct tax from your income every month, so it may be the case that at tax time, all of a sudden you are going to have to remit several thousand dollars to the government in taxes owed. If you don't save for that, you are going to get yourself into a debt-and-interest situation. You might have to pay back the tax money you owe in instalments to the government, and just like a credit card, the government will charge you interest on the money you owe; or you may decide to put that debt on a credit card, which will obviously also include being charged interest.

The best advice may be to get yourself a certified professional personal and corporate income tax accountant up front, who can help advise you as to what expenses can be "written-off" (forgiven to reduce the total amount of money you can say that you cleared/earned that year). An accountant can estimate or forecast for you, based on your particular circumstances, the approximate amount you will likely owe at year end. Think about setting up a tax account with the government and making monthly tax payments. Paying a tax bill quarterly (every three months) is hard. You might not save it up properly, or find an emergency or luxury expense you'd prefer to spend the money on.

As well, if you're running your own business, you'll have to pay into the mandatory Canada Pension Plan so that when you're old and retire, you'll have a small amount of money coming in to you every month. But beware: **THIS IS NOT ENOUGH MONEY TO LIVE ON**, and some are afraid that it may not even actually be available to us once time passes and we get old and retire. Oh, and guess what? When you are old and getting your monthly pension plan cheque payments, you are likely going to end up losing some of it to income taxes. **SO YOU NEED TO SIMULTANEOUSLY INVEST IN AN ADDITIONAL SAVINGS PLAN** *now* **FOR YOUR FUTURE.**

Owing More Tax than Is Taken off Your Paycheque

If you're one of those people who end up with a steady company or government job, the employer will deduct taxes off each of your paycheques. You may think this monthly or biweekly tax deduction is going to cover you, but SURPRISE — sometimes at the end of the taxation year you find out that you actually still owe the government more taxes (for a variety of reasons that I am not qualified to outline). For example, issues can arise if you live in a border city and work in one province and live in another. The way you get around this is to ask your pay advisor to actually deduct *more* tax from each paycheque. The thing is that if you overpay, you don't lose that money. You will be reimbursed in the form of a tax refund. Someone who lives on his or her own is a much more mobile person in that it's easier for him/her to move to other provinces or territories. If you pay extra throughout the year and decide to move to another province or territory, you might just cover yourself against paying a higher tax rate at the end of the year in your new area of residence.

Should you be so lucky as to get a tax refund from overpayment, you can use it to pay down a debt, pay toward tuition, buy an investment instrument, or pay for something extravagant like a vacation getaway, clothes, gadgets, etc.

Some Provinces/Territories Are Taxed at Higher Rates

Besides federal taxes, there are also provincial/territorial taxes. You will probably notice on your paycheque that there are "federal" as well as "provincial/territorial" deductions. If you are a single person with no children, some provinces/territories will be more expensive for you to live in because the taxation system is set up to be more highly in favour of supporting families with children. There, the plan is to increase the birth rate, hence the population (from which they will eventually be able to receive more money through taxation). Some places are doubly taxed compared to others. You can call the appropriate provincial/territorial tax collection agency and ask what the tax rate is for a person earning your level of income. Some provinces/territories are cooler and they have more services, so you might decide it's worth it for you to pay high taxes and live there anyway. That's the reality nobody tells you outright, though.

The Effect of Municipal Taxes on the Cost of Rent

In addition to federal and provincial/territorial taxes, there are also municipal taxes, which are charged to homeowners. This is one of the reasons why homeowners charge high rent rates: so that they can cover the rise in property taxes charged by the city, for example.

Okay, okay! Enough about the dreaded taxes already . . . Moving On!

Eco-friendly Living

Public Transportation

Public transit is one of the best and cheapest ways to get around Canada's major cities and it is obviously a greener choice than everyone having her/his own car. In addition to being the best ecological choice for mass transit, on a practical level it is way cheaper than having your own car, since owning a car means making payments to buy or lease a car, cover the costs associated with paying for car insurance, driving and licence plate permits, clean-drive vehicle emission testing, gasoline, parking costs, mechanical repairs, new tires, etc. However, sometimes we need a car. Consider joining an auto-share program, which most cities have. This is an excellent way to rent a car at a reasonable rate.

The Bicycle

The bicycle is obviously the greenest transportation choice beyond walking! When choosing to be a cyclist, please consider how essential a bike helmet is. You only have one brain; have you ever seen the hardships experienced by people with a head injury? It's certainly life-altering in the worst way for the individual and for family and friends.

All your thoughts and dreams and actions come from impulses that arise from your brain. Your ability to be independent and to earn a living for yourself is largely dependent upon your having an intact brain without injury. It deserves a lot of respect and protection. (Incidentally, this is why drugs and excessive alcohol are a bad choice, too, as they can permanently damage your brain.) Beyond the helmet, it's worth it to spend a bit of money to create the ultimate commuter bicycle. Consider getting a bell, light, splash guards on the front and back wheel, Velcro straps to stop your pant legs from getting caught in the chain, and a bike rack and bike bags to put your stuff in. These additions make riding your bike a very pleasant and reasonable mode of transportation. Watch out for the "door prize" (car doors opening)! Drivers are not always cognizant that they are sharing the road with cyclists, and between a car and a cyclist, the cyclist is always on the losing end of the ordeal.

The best country in the world for cycling is The Netherlands (Holland) — check it out if you can. Cyclists have their own separate bike lanes on all roads and even have their own traffic lights. I sure wish Canada would make it a legal requirement that all new roads have a dedicated bike lane. It would make for a more healthy society, people, and planet.

Commuting by bicycle, if you have a safe enough route, can be an amazing way to get around, improve your fitness, breathe fresh air, get some sunlight, hear birds singing, and see the flowers grow. We've lost a lot of socialization by becoming a major car society. Life goes so fast, and our experiences become increasingly individualistic rather than inclusive of societal exchange. See if you can figure out what I mean. If it seems right, ride past people with a smile and perhaps even saying a friendly hello. Most Canadians will respond positively!

Recycling and Composting

Large Canadian cities have great recycling programs for your paper, plastic, metal, and glass materials. Many, like Ottawa, Toronto, and Vancouver also have composting programs to turn your fruit and veggie detritus into beautiful, fertile soil. Take full advantage of these programs to help all of us reduce the amount of garbage piling up in Canadian landfills.

If you want to be super-adventurous, you might consider composting by vermiculture. This is basically where you put a container inside your home with soil and other materials and select worm varieties that will be very happy to eat your food compost. There are a few tricks to doing it right.

When I first started my homemade bin system, I wasn't making the worms happy so I would come home and find dead worms that had tried to escape (Yes, I know that's totally gross!). They crawled out, dried out, and died somewhere mid-living room floor. So sorry, I was a worm slum landlord — R.I.P., worms! In the end, I figured out that placing my vermiculture bin, without a lid, in the darkness of the cupboard under the kitchen counter was what they liked. Worms actually need a lot of oxygen, and the lid I had used to close the bin was a) causing too much humidity to build up, and b) depriving them of the oxygen they needed. Although it sounds scary not to put a lid on top, they were happy to manoeuvre around in the soil and eat and they just didn't crawl out. With one batch of worms, to get the whole thing started, I had that bin going effectively for three years until the soil got infested with moths (not sure why and I'm sure you really don't need the details on that!). In the end, I just returned the soil and the worms to the outdoor garden, and I'm sure the worms were quite happy to have an expanded travel zone!

Worms and top-of-the-line vermiculture bins can be purchased and shipped anywhere in Canada by visiting *www.capitalwormranch.com*. To access further information and visual images on vermiculture, visit *www.cityfarmer.org/wormcomp61.html*.

Disposing of Batteries and Light Bulbs

Throwing out batteries and light bulbs is not exactly easy for us. Unfortunately we don't have convenient city-run pickup programs to safely dispose of these hazardous items we use every day. If you are really a keener, you can Google your city and figure out how your municipal (city) government will collect these items. In the Google search line, enter something like, "City of Regina battery disposal," or "City of Toronto battery recycling." Most cities have designated areas where you can go and drop off these hazardous materials.

Batteries

Just about all cities are recommending that rechargeable batteries be purchased by consumers. That advice makes sense ecologically and economically. In addition to city locations, many stores will accept your rechargeable battery disposal, such as some Staples Canada/Business Depot, Home Depot, Rona, Pharmasave, and The Source stores. The Web site *www.call2recycle.org* has a "Recycling at Home" section on the home page that you click on, which takes you to a page that has an option to "Find a location nearest you." By entering a Toronto postal code, I saw 459 options for stores to take my batteries to. By entering a postal code in Winnipeg, I saw 55 stores.

Light Bulbs

Again, it's tricky. Some stores like Canadian Tire, Home Depot, Ikea, and Rona will accept your incandescent light bulbs and tubes. Call your local store to ask if they'll accept your disposal items before you make a trip. Consider taking your bulbs back to the store or city-run drop-off point in the packaging it came in, so that they don't break and injure anyone.

Plastic, Mesh, and Cloth Bags

Most people would agree that plastic bags are an enemy of:

- The earth (if bags break down before 1,000 years, their chemicals leach into the soil)
- Birds (they can get tangled in plastic, especially those thin plastic produce bags or those mesh bags used to contain onions or avocados)
- Oceans (the amount of plastic floating in the oceans is despicable)
- Water creatures (e.g., turtles, dolphins, and whales eat plastic bags thinking they are jellyfish; the bags get caught in their stomachs and make them sick and they die)

We live in the modern age, and it is true that having a small number of plastic bags is useful. Having a large number is not environmentally responsible.

According to *www.greenerfootprints.com*, Canadians use from nine to fifteen billion plastic bags a year (YIKES)! That is not cool.

When you see a large variance in an estimate like that, you might question the validity of the estimate, but even any number in the billions is very bad. If you want some old-school information, my grandmother said that in Winnipeg before the plastic bag days (obviously many moons ago, since she's now ninety-two), they used to wrap indoor garbage in newspaper and put it out in the outdoor garbage bin in the back alley. Perhaps that's something you might like to consider, especially when it's winter (garbage is less prone to attract animals if it's frozen).

It is a worthy endeavour to shop using cloth bags. Many cloth bags made today are strong and are rectangular in shape (which helps the groceries pack better). They look relatively cool — and you look like a cool person for using them! The black-coloured ones from Loblaws are especially great because they don't get scuffed up and dirty fast, either on the inside or the outside.

Buying a set of fine cloth mesh bags for putting fruits and veggies in is infinitely better than using the very thin film plastic bags. Those thin plastic bags are apparently among the worst offenders to the earth and to marine animals. You just wash out the fine mesh bags by throwing them in with your laundry or washing them with your dishes. Try having a look at buying them through this Canadian company: *www.carebagsonline.com*. These would make great Christmas or birthday gifts for people who have everything or for the eco-conscious, hopefully including yourself!

Consider challenging yourself to buy only one box of 100 zippable sandwich bags in a year. The plastics industry prides itself in the indestructible nature of its product. You can recognize this inherent quality and wash the zippable sandwich bag after using it. Hang it to dry on the silverware or on top of a glass in the dish drainer so that it can dry out. It works! If you think about it, 100 bags in a year is actually a lot for a single person. In general, try not to be a bag hoarder who stuffs tons of plastic bags in the cupboard under the kitchen counter! (Yes, I've been there, done that, but a person can evolve!)

Soaps for Dishes, Laundry, Shampoo, etc.

Environmentally friendly dish and laundry soap actually do work well. They are just advertised less on TV and usually don't have the fancy (toxic) colourants, scents, and other chemicals added to them. Some people enjoy shampoos and toothpaste from the health-food stores. Be a kind person to the earth and try replacing some of the mainstream stuff with environmentally friendly options so that chemicals don't get dumped out into the lakes, rivers, or oceans and kill the marine animals and water plants (and contaminate our drinking water).

Of course, these are only the basics, along with keeping all lights off that you aren't using and avoiding "vampire" usage by unplugging the appliances that aren't in use (such as your chargers, hair dryer, DVD player, TV, etc.) because they still draw power when they are not "on." (I'm still totally working on this one! I'm not the "greenest" person around.) Please engage your creativity and think of other ways to be a Canadian who lives a little greener!

Gardening with Indigenous Plants

If you should be lucky enough to rent a place with a front yard, a backyard, or a balcony, you might consider making an effort to plant indigenous flowers, trees, herbs, and plants that are native to your ecological area. This will give bees, other pollinators like butterflies, and native wildlife opportunities to have appropriate food and shelter sources (are you singing the "Hinterland Who's Who" song?). You can also have an impact on making our environment greener and the air cleaner! To research suitable gardening options, visit *www.evergreen.ca* or *www.wildaboutgardening.org*.

Living with the World

C anada is home to the demographics of the whole world. Our country includes indigenous peoples (First Nations, Métis, and Inuit) who have always lived here in Canada, before all the other immigrants arrived, as well as new citizens and descendants from every part of the globe. As a point of interest, "Canada" is a word derived from "Kanata" from the Huron-Iroquoian language, which means village. Many of Canada's location names are also derived from indigenous languages, such as: "Saskatchewan," which is a match to a Cree word meaning, "fast-flowing river." William Commanda, a respected

Algonquin First Nation elder, once told me that the word "Quebecois" is the sound of the way the Algonquin people say "hello, stranger."

Canada is one of the safest, most culturally advanced, and accepting nations on the planet. Although overt and subtle racism certainly still do exist here, it is a Canadian principle that we strive to welcome, accept, and appreciate the cultural uniqueness and differences of our fellow citizens. Your neighbourhood will likely include a great mix of people from different cultures or a concentration of people with a certain cultural heritage.

Some researchers and media like to make a point of mentioning that Canadian cities are changing from the "visible minorities" to the "visible majority," where our citizens with darker skin complexions are increasing in population. My question is: So what? Consider that when the people of darker-coloured skin are those who are counted as being part of Canada's "new cultural demographic," it is overlooked that cultures with fair skin are totally highly varied as well. For example: Russian, Hungarian, Italian, Macedonian, Bulgarian, Swedish, Estonian, Polish, Greek, Spanish, French, Dutch, Australian, Scottish people, etc., are all people whose cultural norms, histories, languages, religions, and spoken accents are as different and as complex as people from Africa, Thailand, China, India, or wherever else.

In Canada, we try our best to respect each other, learn from each other, enjoy each other's foods and cultural expressions, etc. Whatever your cultural background is, whether you feel bi-cultural or just "Canadian," trust and believe that you belong here, because you do! (It goes without saying that the indigenous people obviously belong here!)

Perhaps you'll have the opportunity to live in a highly multicultural Canadian urban neighbourhood, or others like "Little Italy" or "Chinatown," or a neighbourhood with a well-established Indian, Korean, or Portuguese community. Maybe you'll expand the typical foods you eat or you'll enjoy a local summer or arts festival celebrating that neighbourhood's majority culture. Living in such neighbourhoods will probably find their own ways of influencing you and your perspectives just a little bit — hopefully in the best way possible.

Summary

- Living on your own can be a satisfying, enjoyable, complex, difficult and rewarding experience.

- There are tricks to doing it well, many of which I've shared with you in this book.

- Consider asking friends and family for additional advice.

- An active social network can be an important component to living well on your own.

- Having the patience and the confidence to experiment and discover your own best ideas for living on your own successfully is a worthy aim and a large part of the fun!

GOOD LUCK!

**MAY YOU ACHIEVE THE BALANCE AND ENJOYMENT
THAT COMES FROM MOVING OUT AND LIVING ON YOUR OWN
IN A BIG CANADIAN CITY.**

APPENDIX A

Residential Tenancy Dispute Resolution Services and Information

G oogle the government department name to get the link to the Web site address. You will find a lot of information and resources to help you learn the parameters of landlord and tenant rights and responsibilities in your province or territory. These departments and agencies are typically open during business hours (8:30 a.m. to 4:30 p.m. or 9 a.m. to 5 p.m.). They can review your claim that you are being treated badly by the landlord. Sometimes they charge a small fee to help you with dispute resolution (approximately forty-five dollars).

Province / Territory	Government Department	Contact Information
Alberta	Service Alberta, Residential Tenancy Dispute Resolution Service	Edmonton: Dial toll free 310–0000 (then 780–644–3000). Calgary: Dial toll free 310–0000 (then 780–644–3000). rtdrs@gov.ab.ca
British Columbia	Ministry of Housing and Social Development, Residential Tenancy Branch	Lower mainland: 604–660–1020 Victoria: 250–387–1602 Elsewhere in B.C.: 1–800–665–8779 HSRTO@gov.bc.ca
Manitoba	Consumer and Corporate Affairs Division, Residential Tenancies Branch	Winnipeg: Tel: 204–945–2476 Toll Free: 1–800–782–8403 rtb@gov.mb.ca Brandon: Tel: 204–726–6230 Toll Free: 1–800–656–8481 rtbbrandon@gov.mb.ca Thompson: Tel: 204–677–6496 Toll Free:1–800–229–0639 rtbthompson@gov.mb.ca

New Brunswick	Service New Brunswick Office of the Rentalsman	Toll free: 1–888–762–8600
Newfoundland and Labrador	Government Services: Residential Tenancies Branch	Toll free: 1–877–829–2608
Northwest Territories	Department of Justice, Rental Office	867–920–8047 or 1–800–661–0760
Nova Scotia	Service Nova Scotia and Municipal Relations, Residential Tenancy	1–800–670–4357
Nunavut	Department of Justice, Residential Tenancies Act	867–975–7291
Ontario	Landlord and Tenant Board	1–888–332–3234, or in Toronto, 416–645–8080
Prince Edward Island	Office of the Director of Residential Rental Property	902–892–3501
Quebec	Régie du logement, Complaints Bureau	1–800–683–2245, or in Montreal, 514–873–2245
Saskatchewan	Justice and Attorney General, Office Residential Tenancies (Rentalsman)	Regina: 306–787–2699 Saskatoon: 306–933–5680 Toll free, province-wide 1–888–215–2222
Yukon	Community Services	867–667–5111

APPENDIX B
MINISTRY OF HEALTH CONTACT NUMBERS

N otify your Ministry of Health when you move.

Alberta	780–427–7164
British Columbia	250–387–6121 604–660–2421 1–800–663–7867
Manitoba	1–866–626–4862
New Brunswick	506–457–4800
Newfoundland and Labrador	709–729–4984
Northwest Territories	1–800–661–0830
Nova Scotia	1–800–387–6665 902–424–5818
Nunavut	Search by location on www.canada411.ca
Ontario	1–866–532–3161
Prince Edward Island	902–368–6130
Quebec	1–877–644–4545 418–644–4545 514–644–4545
Saskatchewan	1–800–667–7766 or 306–787–0146
Yukon	1–800–661–0408 or 867–667–5209

APPENDIX C
CREDIT AND BUDGET COUNSELLING AGENCIES

When you are having a rough time managing to live within your financial means, you may wish to go to an agency to assist you with credit and budget counselling. These organizations typically give you confidential advice and support to help you develop a solid plan to reduce and repay your debts, stop calls from collection agencies, and avoid bankruptcy.

Alberta	403–265–2201
British Columbia	1–888–527–8999
Manitoba	204–942–8789
New Brunswick	1–888–753–2227
Newfoundland and Labrador	1–888–753–2227
Northwest Territories	1–888–294–0076 or 1–888–527–8999
Nova Scotia	1–888–753–2227
Nunavut	1–888–294–0076 or 1–888–527–8999
Ontario	1–888–424–3093
Prince Edward Island	1–888–753–2227
Quebec	514–989–3715 or 1–866–615–1226
Saskatchewan	1–888–215–2222
Yukon	1–888–527–8999

APPENDIX D
FUNERAL INFORMATION / MEMORIAL ADVISORY SOCIETIES

Funeral information / memorial advisory societies are networks of individuals who can talk you through end-of-life issue planning for yourself or a family member. Buying an inexpensive membership can typically give you access to the price lists of funeral services, which are very hard to find for comparison when you are not a member. (The author has included as many societies as she could find.)

ALBERTA

Calgary: *www.calgarymemorial.com/* 1–800–566–9959 or 403–248–2044

Edmonton: *www.memorialsocietyedmonton.ca* 780–944–0196

Red Deer: 403–340–1021 or 403–346–9617

BRITISH COLUMBIA

www.memorialsocietybc.org 1–888–816–5902 or 604–733–7705

MANITOBA

204–452–7999

NOVA SCOTIA

http://memorialsocietynovascotia.wikispaces.com

ONTARIO

Federation of Ontario Memorial Societies: *www.myfuneralplan.org/*

Hamilton: *www.hwcn.org/link/fashd/*

London: *www.londonmemorialsociety.com/*

Ottawa and Eastern Ontario: *http://fiso.ncf.ca/*

Sudbury & Northern Ontario: *www.memorialsociety.ca* 1–866–203–5139 or 705–671–3753

Toronto: *www.fams.ca*

Windsor: *www3.sympatico.ca/stanmcdo/memsoc*

QUEBEC

Montreal: 514–933–8444

SASKATCHEWAN

1–866–283–2677 or 306–374–5190

APPENDIX E

SUICIDE PREVENTION

*T*he author has included as many support numbers as she could find. Many provinces have local area suicide prevention support. To find a specific number in your area, visit the Canadian Association for Suicide Prevention Web site *www.casp-acps.ca/* or call 204–784–4073.

Alberta	Calgary: 1–800–SUICIDE or 1–800–784–2433	24 hours
British Columbia	Province-wide 1–800–SUICIDE or 1–800–784–2433	24 hours
Manitoba	1–877–435–7170	24 hours
New Brunswick	1–800–667–5005 or 506–450–HELP (4357)	24 hours
Newfoundland and Labrador	1–888–737–4668 or 709–737–4668	24 hours
Northwest Territories	1–800–661–0844	7 p.m.–11 p.m. 7 days a week
Nova Scotia	1–888–429–8167 or 902–429–8167	20 hours 9 a.m.–5 a.m.
Nunavut and Nunavik (Arctic Quebec)	Nunavuat Kamatsiaqtut Help Line 1–800–265–3333 or 867–979–3333	7 p.m.–11 p.m. 7 days a week
Nunavut only	Awareness Centre (temporary RCMP crisis line) 867–982–0123	24 hours
Ontario	Ontario does not have a province-wide support line. Google the Ontario Association for Suicide Prevention to find a crisis number in your city or call 911.	
Prince Edward Island	1–800–218–2885	24 hours
Quebec	1–866–277–3553 or 418–683–4588	24 hours
Saskatchewan	306–933–6200	24 hours
Yukon	1–867–668–5733	24 hours

APPENDIX F
ADDICTION TREATMENT SUPPORT

DRUG AND ALCOHOL REHAB CANADA can help connect you with treatment rehabilitation services by substance abuse—city, province, or territory *www.addictionenders.com* or 1-800-419-7941.

CANADIAN CENTRE ON SUBSTANCE ABUSE: *www.ccsa.ca* offers directories to substance and gambling helplines in Canada. General Inquiries: 613-235-4048.

DIRECTORY OF CANADA GAMBLING ADDICTION TREATMENT PROGRAMS:

www.canadadrugrehab.ca/Gambling-Addiction-Treatment.html

APPENDIX G
TAXES

THE CANADA REVENUE AGENCY (CRA) is the Canadian government agency that collects our taxes. If you have any questions, call the CRA (1-800-959-8281). When you move, you should inform the CRA of your new address so that you can get your voter registration card for the next election.

H & R BLOCK® has 1,110 tax service offices across Canada to help people complete their annual income tax returns. Check out their amazingly inexpensive student rates to see if you qualify. Visit *www.hrblock.ca* and use the "Find an Office" button on the top right of the Web site to find an office near you.

CERTIFIED GENERAL ACCOUNTANTS can help you file your income tax returns. They can be found in your city by visiting *www.yellowpages.ca* and by typing your city name and searching "certified general accountant."

APPENDIX H
MOVING

The **CANADIAN ASSOCIATION OF MOVERS** (*www.mover.net*) advises consumers (those moving) of credible moving companies. There is a list you can look up on the Web site. The site also lists advisories and public alerts on bad moving companies.

The **BETTER BUSINESS BUREAU** (*www.bbb.org/canada*) is a service you should use to check out a moving company to see whether or not there have been complaints or whether the moving company appears to be in good standing with the Better Business Bureau.

MOVING BOXES AND SUPPLIES

- *www.movingboxes.ca* or 613–822–6900
- **Wal-Mart** (in the summer months)
- **PODS:** *www.pods.com* or 877–770–7637

ROOMMATE FINDER

http://ca.roommates.com/ and *www.roommates.ca* are excellent Web sites to help you see brief personal descriptions and photos of potential roommates and photos of the living accommodations.

USED FURNITURE

Google Kijiji to see if there is one available in your city or check out sites like *www.usedottawa.com* or *www.usedregina.com*.

About the Author

(Photo courtesy of Sujata Verma)

Cindy Babyn was born in Toronto, Ontario, and proudly wears her love for Canada on her sleeve. She particularly enjoys many aspects of Canadian cultural expression. While acquiring a degree in music performance, she worked with a mentor to influence the University of Toronto's Faculty of Music to celebrate Canadian contemporary music by founding and directing the annual New Music Festival, which continues to exist today.

Since graduating, she has worked to support Canadian musicians' concert series, taught music at a private inner-city music school, and has given it all she's got to further the public good through her various jobs in the Government of Canada (festival and performing arts series support — particularly making a significant impact on the increase in arts funding to First Nations, Métis, and Inuit communities in Ontario; cultural infrastructure support; Canadian cultural exporters support; and foreign direct investment promotion).

Although now and then she has performed as a professional musician in a variety of engagements across Canada, she has allowed that aspect of herself to sunset. In her personal life, she is a visual artist, creating oil paintings of Canadian landscapes, and has taken up ballroom dance lessons. She has dreams of seeing an owl in the wild and flying with a jet pack, just as soon as they become available!

Cindy Babyn has lived in the following locations (sometimes multiple locations in the same neighbourhood), all of which has contributed to the expertise she developed around moving: Toronto (The Beaches, The Annex, Christie Pitts, Regal Heights, Seaton Village, the Financial District); Ottawa (Nepean, The Glebe); Quebec (Gatineau, Chelsea); The Netherlands (four locations in Rotterdam); and Spain (Vilanova i la Geltrú, near Barcelona).

TO ORDER MORE COPIES:

GENERAL STORE PUBLISHING HOUSE

499 O'Brien Road, Box 415, Renfrew, Ontario, Canada K7V 4A6
Tel 1.800.465.6072 • Fax 1.613.432.7184
www.gsph.com